*After*LIFF

JOHN LLOYD wrote *The Meaning of Liff* with Douglas Adams in 1983. He is the original producer of *The News Quiz*, *To the Manor Born*, *Not the Nine O'Clock News*, *Blackadder*, *Spitting Image* and *QI*. He has also produced many books, including *The Book of General Ignorance*, which has been translated into thirty languages. Married to Sarah, they have three little kelks and twelve prospidnicks.

JON CANTER is the author of the comic novels *Seeds of Greatness*, *A Short Gentleman* and *Worth*. He was script editor for *Fry & Laurie*, wrote stand-up with Lenny Henry and his journalism has appeared in the *Guardian*. His radio series *Believe It* won Best Scripted Comedy at the BBC Audio Awards. He lives in Suffolk with the painter Helen Napper and their yafford.

also by John Lloyd (with Douglas Adams)

THE MEANING OF LIFF
THE DEEPER MEANING OF LIFF

also by John Lloyd (with John Mitchinson)

THE BOOK OF GENERAL IGNORANCE
THE SECOND BOOK OF GENERAL IGNORANCE
THE BOOK OF ANIMAL IGNORANCE
ADVANCED BANTER: THE QI BOOK OF QUOTATIONS
THE QI BOOK OF THE DEAD
THE QI 'E', 'F', 'G' & 'H' ANNUALS

also by John Lloyd (with John Mitchinson
& James Harkin)

1,227 QI FACTS TO BLOW YOUR SOCKS OFF

also by Jon Canter published by Vintage

SEEDS OF GREATNESS
A SHORT GENTLEMAN
WORTH

After LIFF

*The New Dictionary
of Things There Should
Be Words For*

JOHN LLOYD
JON CANTER

ff

faber and faber

First published in the UK in 2013
by Faber and Faber Ltd
Bloomsbury House
74–77 Great Russell Street
London WC1B 3DA

Typeset by Faber and Faber Ltd
Printed in England by CPI Group (UK) Ltd, Croydon, CR0 4YY

A CIP record for this book
is available from the British Library

ISBN 978-0-571-30169-0

2 4 6 8 10 9 7 5 3 1

To DNA, our friend

CONTENTS

CONTENTS

FOREWORD by Jon Lloyd

FOREWORD by John Lloyd

It's thirty years since Douglas Adams and I wrote *The Meaning of Liff* and, four years later, *The Deeper Meaning of Liff*.

That they're both still in print is a testament to the simplicity and universal appeal of the idea: that all sorts of perfectly common things around us have somehow escaped having names, and that this can be easily remedied by recycling the ones on signposts.

It's a game anyone can play, and many do. Since Douglas's tragic death at the absurdly young age of forty-nine, his friends and admirers have gone on adding to his legacy by inventing new liffs – on his website h2g2.com, on my website qi.com, on Twitter's @ThatsLiff, and in various competitions over the years run by his indefatigable brother James to raise money for Douglas's favourite charity, Save the Rhino.

Early in 2013, as a celebration of the original work, Radio 4 broadcast *The Meaning of*

Liff at 30. Listeners' own submissions were invited and this again produced a rich new crop of liffs. Just as it seemed a waste to have words cluttering up signposts when they could be usefully attached to something namelessly familiar, so it seemed an equal waste not to make use of all this public creativity. This book is the result. Many, many people have had a hand in it, and you can find their names (under my grateful thanks) in the acknowledgements at the back.

But there is one name, above all, to whom *Afterliff* owes its existence, that of my co-author, Jon Canter. Of course, nothing and no one can ever replace Douglas – his brilliance, his originality, his joyous genius – but when it comes to penning liffs at least, Jon comes awfully close.

The three of us were at university together and remained lifelong friends until that terrible day in 2001 when Douglas had his heart attack. Back in the 1970s, Jon and I had both, at different times, shared flats with Douglas and, in the eighties, Jon became the third (shamefully uncredited) author of *The Deeper Meaning of Liff*. He proved at once to be a master of the genre, coming up with many of the best lines – including three of the six chosen for the *Deeper* back cover. His contribution to that book was incalculable, as it is to this.

We both hope you have as much fun reading *Afterliff* as we had writing it and, to Douglas, in whichever universe he may be, we say, 'So Long, and Thanks for All the Liffs'.

JOHN LLOYD
Hammersmith, May 2013

Aachen n.
The fake name you add to the front of your mobile phone's address book to stop answering the *aasi* (q.v.).

Aasi n.
The first person in a mobile phone's address book, who gets all the calls from handbags and pockets.

Ab Lench excl./ph.
Not up for anything, quite literally – the opposite of 'gung ho'.

Abbots Ripton n.
Man in a dog collar at a party who you're sure doesn't really believe in all that God stuff.

Abcott n.
The tiny remnant of a bar of soap.

A

Aachen *n.*
The fake name you add to the front of your
mobile phone's address book to stop annoying
the aast (q.v.).

Aast *n.*
The first person in a mobile phone's address
book, who gets all the calls from handbags
and pockets.

Ab Lench *adj.phr.*
Not up for anything much, really: the opposite
of 'gung ho'.

Abbots Ripton *n.*
Man in a dog collar at a party who tells you he
'doesn't really believe in all that God stuff'.

Abcott *n.*
The tiny remnant of a bar of soap.

Aberdovey *n.*
A tribute band composed mostly of pigeons.

Aberglasney *n.*
The particular kind of self-pity induced by alcohol.

Aberlemno *n.*
The little shelf on a tennis umpire's stepladder where the soft drinks are kept.

Abernethy *n.*
Unit of fluffiness. In five-star hotels, the white towels and dressing gowns must be a minimum of 90 abernethy.

Acaster Malbis *n.*
One who stands at a pelican crossing, watches you press the WAIT button, and then presses it again.

Adbolton *n.*
Short, fast, baffling burst of sponsorship repeated either side of the commercial breaks in a TV show till it drives viewers mad.

Addison *n.*
The extra time you need to allow when taking
a shortcut.

Adjungbilly *n.*
The ring of discarded leaflets on the
pavement a few feet from the person handing
them out.

Ae *n.*
Useful two-letter Scrabble word: a player who
has drawn nothing but vowels.

Agharoo *n.*
A larger-than-life sneeze in a Bollywood
comedy, used as the basis for a dance routine.

Aismunderby *n.*
The dent on either side of the nose of a
person who wears glasses.

Alawoona *n.*
A sacred chant for the wellbeing of the Dow
Jones Index.

Albox *n.*
A mail-order package that arrives but appears not to weigh anything.

Alkipi *n.*
Japanese thank-you-letter-writing torture.

Almurta *n.*
Code of silence among pets that stops your parrot from telling you what your cat just did on your bed.

Alvechurch *n.*
A place of worship in which the clergy outnumber the congregation.

Amazonia *pl.n.*
Small last-minute gifts ordered online to top up a main present that the giver suspects won't be good enough on its own.

Amby *adj.*
Reluctant to be the first to slag someone off but happy to join in as things hot up.

Amcotts *pl.n.*
Orange-tipped cotton buds found behind
things in the bathroom.

Amesbury *n.*
The legal process by which a judge in a
divorce case decides who gets custody of the
couple's friends.

Ancaster *n.*
A name on a building with one of its letters
missing.

Ando *n.*
The art of mastering Japanese toilets.

Anembo *adv.*
The way creative directors and
commissioning editors sit: leaning back with
their hands behind their head and their feet
on the desk.

Anglesey *n.*
Hypothetical object at which a lazy eye is
looking.

Annagry *adj.*
Infuriated by the last crossword clue.

Annecy *n.*
A half-sucked Tic Tac or jellybean found
sticking to a pair of sunglasses in the glove
compartment.

Anthorn *n.*
(MEDICAL) A penis so embarrassingly small
that the doctor secretly takes a picture of it
on his phone.

Antist *n.*
A vet who specialises in insects.

Antrim *n.*
Barber's term for the unmentionable hair
discreetly snipped from eyebrows, nostrils
and earholes.

Arbroath *n.*
Throat-clearing
designed to alert
passers-by to your
presence in the
lavatory.

Arbuckle Junction *n.*
That point in the task where you realise it's
going to be a lot harder than you thought.

Ardateggle *v.*
To poke burning pornography into the tiniest
possible fragments.

Arkansas *n.*
Any name not pronounced the way it's spelt.

Aruba *n.*
Small bottle of scented liquid in a hotel
bathroom that could be shampoo, moisturiser,
disinfectant or liqueur.

Ashby Puerorum *n.*
One who prefaces every utterance with 'In my
day . . .'

Askamore *n.*
An Italian waiter who keeps coming back to
find out if everything's all right.

Askham Bryan *n.*
The junior journalist despatched to the scene
of a disaster to gather answers to the question
'How do you feel?'

Asquith *n.*
Person in a doctor's waiting room who appears
to have absolutely nothing wrong with them.

Aston Clinton *n.*
Clean-cut American student destined to
become a partner in a corrupt legal firm.

Attunga *n.*
The ding that tells you the lift has arrived.

Attymon *n.*
A West Indian cricket enthusiast.

Audley End *n.*
The sentence you read in bed and read in bed
again and read in bed again and then your
eyes close.

Aughnaloopy *n.*
A tangle of tights and bras.

Avening *ptcpl.v.*
Putting on your coat to say goodbye, then
spending fifteen minutes saying it.

Avonmouth *n.*
A woman who has overdone her lipstick.

B

Babeary n.
A front papoose ostentatiously worn by full-time fathers.

Badger-Bloat n.
The sexual position you know nothing about despite your partner's eagerness to try it.

Badlesmere n.
One who dishonestly ticks the 'I have read and agree to the Terms and Conditions' box.

Baffle n.
Hearty squeeze of an acquaintance's testicles, otherwise known as a 'South African' handshake.

Baghela n.
Modish variety of Milanese pizza shaped like a little man-satchel.

B

Babcary *n.*
A front papoose ostentatiously worn by first-time fathers.

Badgers Mount *n.*
The sexual position you knew wouldn't work despite your partner's eagerness to try it.

Badlesmere *n.*
One who dishonestly ticks the 'I have read and agree to the Terms and Conditions' box.

Baffie *n.*
Hearty squeeze of an acquaintance's testicles, otherwise known as a 'South African handshake'.

Baghetti *n.*
Modish variety of Milanese pasta shaped like little man-satchels.

Balerno *n.*
The spooky sensation that someone is about to explain *déjà vu* to you.

Ballywatticock *n.*
Someone who brings his own clubs to seaside Crazy Golf.

Balmaha *adv.*
With hands on hips and feet wide apart; the stance of city dwellers appreciating the view at weekends.

Balranald *n.*
One who phones up in a rage to complain about a show they didn't watch.

Baltyfarrell *n.*
A table with one leg shorter than the others.

Bambill *n.*
The 'Back in 5 Mins' sign on a shop door that's been there over an hour.

Banada *n.*
A Canadian banana.

Bangkok *n.*
A dud firework found in a flowerbed.

Bankhead *n.*
One who quits a highly paid job in the
City to become a gardener, potter, baker or
hypnotherapist.

Bannerbank *n.*
The void above the human shoulder that
anthropologists believe evolved to leave room
for TV graphics or video clips.

Barbaggio *n.*
The tourist place you go to for the first meal of
your holiday because you don't yet know any
better.

Barbican *n.*
The reflection of a street lamp on a car roof
on a rainy night, which looks like a taxi sign
until you try to flag it down.

Barcillonnette *n.*
The beep of a supermarket till as it scans an
item.

Barjarg *n.*
The uncomfortable seating in fast-food restaurants, designed to make you eat the food faster.

Barlin *n.*
The hand gesture, with thumb to ear and little finger to mouth, which signals you'd like someone to call you.

Barnave *n.*
A man who addresses groups of women as 'guys'.

Barnawartha *n.*
State of grace achieved by finally freeing your cafetière of all grounds.

Barooga *n.*
Nervous twitch of a dog startled by the sudden and unexpected recoiling of a metal tape measure.

Barwick-in-Elmet *n.*
Lusty knight undergoing voluntary chastity to work up a keen sense of rage before battle.

Basket Swamp *n.*
A beach café dripping with wet swimmers.

Bawtry *adj.*
Uneasy from standing in a tepid pool of someone else's shower water.

Beagle Gulf *n.*
The time in years, months, days, hours and minutes since a lapsed smoker last had a cigarette.

Beattock *n.*
The part of someone's body you stroke seductively in bed, only to discover it's not the part you thought it was.

Beaucroissant *n.*
Male flatmate who spends all his time in the bathroom.

Beausemblant *n.*
One who expects to be understood in France
if he speaks English with a French accent.

Bebeah *n.*
The delicious aroma of a baby's head.

Beelsby *n.*
A leg or antenna of an insect suspended in a
jar of clear honey.

Beeston *n.*
A low-pitched drone,
as from an unseen
motorway or history
teacher.

Bejoording *ptcpl.v.*
Exaggerating a footballer's sexual prowess to
increase the value of a kiss-and-tell story.

Belltrees *pl.n.*
The numbered options you're offered by an
automated answering service, none of which
you want.

Belmont *n.*
An alarm clock cast in a starring role in a
dream.

Belmunging *ptcpl.v.*
Passing on gossip divulged to you on
condition it went no further, on the strict
understanding that it goes no further.

Beltana *n.*
A canapé you consume in one go without
having any idea what it is.

Bempton *n.*
A complete stranger who inexplicably singles
you out for a buffeting on the dodgems.

Bermuda *n.*
The last remaining, least popular chocolate in
the box.

Big Neeston *n.*
A Scotsman everyone agrees with on account
of his size.

Biggleswade *n.*
What leather flying jackets are lined with.

Binegar *n.*
Any liquid left in a jar in the fridge for so long that it's separated into two or more components.

Bingley *n.*
One who announces his presence in a room by making jaunty noises.

Birtle *v.*
To make something worse by trying to improve it.

Biscathorpe *n.*
Collection of old patterned tins on top of your grandmother's fridge.

Bishop's Nympton *n.*
The curly bit on the end of a bishop's staff, which he uses to gather cobwebs or tickle the congregation.

Blaby *n.*
A balloon that refuses to inflate, no matter how hard you blow into it.

[18]

Blargies *pl.n.*
The smatterings of food that fly onto the mirror when you floss.

Blindcrake *v.*
To fumble under the dashboard for the bonnet release.

Boasley Cross *n.*
An encounter between two enemies in the street, in which they nod to each other as they pass, count to five, and then mutter 'Arsehole'.

Bodelwyddan *adj.*
Unable to walk straight after getting off a playground roundabout.

Bodnant *n.*
The perky little fellow at a distant relative's funeral who seems to know who you are.

Boffles *n.*
High-waisted trousers worn by old men.

Bogue *n.*
Something not, and never likely to be, in vogue. 'The bogue for dip-dyed culottes will continue this season. Be seen with them and die.' *Tatler*

Boloquoy *n.*
Rambling monologue cursing yourself the morning after behaving badly.

Boufflers *pl.n.*
Strangers who say 'Oo, he's gorgeous!' as they smile at your baby daughter.

Bowlish *adj.*
Impatient to get to the dessert course.

Bowshank *n.*
A lavatory set so close to the cistern that the seat won't stand up on its own.

Boxworth *n.*
A person who can't enter a room without turning on a TV or radio.

Boyanup *n.*
The perverse rush of pleasure you get the first
time your son beats you fair and square at
tennis.

Bracknell *v.*
To explain patiently to an older person how to
use a computer.

Brampton Bierlow *n.*
The chuntering noise made by an old
photocopier to let you know it's thinking
about doing something.

Bricy *adj.*
Worryingly inexpensive.

Briffons *pl.n.*
Bare-bottomed garden gnomes; men's
aprons with breasts
on; chocolate
penises; tinned
panties.

BRIXWORTH 2
NORTHAMPTON 8

Brightlingsea *n.*
The blinding rush of light when someone opens the curtains in the morning before you're ready.

Brighton *n.*
The little light that tells you a piece of electrical equipment is working.

Bringolo *interj.*
Cry of admiration in an Italian restaurant, when a waiter carrying four plates bursts through the kitchen door.

Briscous *adj.*
Bewilderingly resilient, as with Jeffrey Archer or the Ebola virus.

Brixham *n.*
A builder who tidies up after himself at the end of the day.

Brixworth *n.*
The extra time you allow yourself in bed when you wake up thinking it's a weekday and then remember it isn't.

Broadwoodwidger *n.*
An eighteenth-century craftsman, maker of
strange fanciful implements designed to be
hung on the walls of taverns as conversation
pieces. In her *History of Broadwoodwidgery*
(2009), Hilary Mann writes: 'It is a tribute to
the enduring craft of the broadwoodwidger
that people still go into pubs in Britain, look
at the objects hanging on the wall and ask,
"What the hell is that?"'

Brombos *interj.*
Traditional cry of a real Mexican
as he bites
into a chilli
pepper.

Brompton Ralph *n.*
A tramp with an upper-class accent.

Broons *pl.n.*
The rubbery beige things in cellophane
envelopes they sell on trains instead of
croissants.

Brouchy *adj.*
Looking at the world through dung-coloured spectacles.

Brulange *n.*
The black dust scraped from burnt toast.

Brund *n.*
The mood you're in when you don't know what mood you're in.

Buding *ptcpl.v.*
Making friends with someone by finding things in common you both dislike.

Bugle Gate *n.*
A sign with attitude, such as 'Don't Even Think of Parking Here' or 'Trespassers Will Be Shot'.

Bulwell *v.*
To successfully argue a point without believing a word of it.

Bunratty *adj.*
Annoyed with yourself for eating too many Krispy Kreme doughnuts.

[24]

Burlats *pl.n.*
Noises from the waking world – footsteps, car horns, doors, belmonts (q.v.) – incorporated into a dream.

Burzy *n.*
A kiss goodnight from your father.

Bussnang *n.*
(ARCHAIC) The bell the conductor rings twice to tell the driver to move off.

Butt of Lewis *n.*
Spin-off television series not featuring the actor who was the reason you watched the original.

Bweeng *n.*
One who cries on cue in soppy movies.

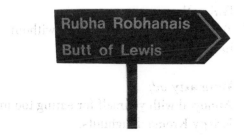

C

Cagnoche-s *pl.n.*
Unsettling square nocturnal earrings.

Campo Grande *adj.*
In the style of Quentin Crisp.

Canuples *pl.n.*
What ducks are looking for once they...

Cappamany *adj.*
Quizzical, belligerent, sideways; the way a
chicken looks at you

Capoth *adj.*
Harmlessly broken, because in use anyway
– e.g. the F11 key on a PC keyboard
or top D sharp on a piano.

Caramay *adj.*
Not seeming tanned till you get back from
holiday and see yourself in a mirror.

C

Cagnoncles *pl.n.*
Unsettling aquatic nocturnal clankings.

Campo Grande *adv.*
In the style of Quentin Crisp.

Canaples *pl.n.*
What ducks are looking for under the water.

Cappananty *adj.*
Quizzical, belligerent, sideways: the way a
chicken looks at you.

Caputh *adj.*
Harmlessly broken, because never used
anyway – e.g. the F11 key on a PC keyboard
or top D sharp on a piano.

Caramany *adj.*
Not seeming tanned till you get back from
holiday and see yourself in a mirror.

Carlops *n.*
A light approaching on a dark road that appears to be a motorcycle but turns out to be a lorry with a missing headlamp.

Carlton Scroop *n.*
The credit card you only use to scrape ice off the windscreen.

Carnalbanagh Sheddings *pl.n.*
The snippets of paper and scrunched-up Sellotape left behind after a present-wrapping session.

Carnforth *interj.*
Insolent yell of weedy ruffians from a safe distance.

Carnoustie *n.*
A baby woodlouse.

Carrogs *pl.n.*
Archaeological remains that are highly significant but look like a bunch of stones.

Carse of Lecropt *n.*
Rectangular Anglo-Saxon receptacle made of
bark and baked mud that scholars believe is
the first box anyone thought outside of.

Cashel *n.*
The bowl in which small useless foreign coins
are kept.

Castleruddery *n.*
Psychological warfare at international-level
chess.

Caterham *n.*
An overwhelming desire to use the Pope's hat
as an oven glove.

Chadbury *n.*
Any jar of
preserves,
chutney or
organic suppository
ointment apparently handmade by
Prince Charles.

CHERRY BURTON

Chambilly n.
Something in the zoo that looks like a goat but isn't.

Chanlockfoot n.
Filmgoer who stays seated through the end credits to show they know what a Best Boy is.

Cherry Burton n.
The rosy pallor of a butcher's face.

Cherry Hinton n.
Remark by a girl in a bar that suggests she might be up for it.

Chertsey v.
To greet someone by half-rising from your seat.

Chetnole n.
The knob on a stopwatch.

Chettle v.
To pat one's pockets while hurrying past beggars.

Chevening *ptcpl.v.*
Rifling through your post in a desperate
search for anything unconnected to charity or
solar panelling.

Chichery *adj.*
Set on edge by the fiddliness of something.

Chinley *adj.*
Gifted with the ability
to use the lower jaw as a
third hand when folding
sheets.

Chudleigh *n.*
An overweight person in a hurry.

Chuffily-Roche *adv.*
The way a banker walks after receiving his
bonus.

Clathy *adj.*
Squeaky clean after a bath.

Clavering *ptcpl.v.*
Pretending to text when alone and feeling
vulnerable in public.

Clayton *n.*
Small trowel-like implement used by cabin crew to apply foundation.

Cleethorpes *pl.n.*
People who wear slogans that run across more than one T-shirt, sit next to each other at public events and cheer if pointed out.

Clent *adj.*
Squeamish about using the C-word.

Cleobury Mortimer *n.*
A person who marries a royal then gets divorced but is probably still worth sucking up to.

Cliasmol *n.*
Short-lived drug, briefly popular in the 1990s, which claimed to cure addiction to Pringles.

Clignancourt *n.*
Group of chattering teenage French tourists who stand on the pavement blocking your way.

Climping *ptcpl.v.*
The accidental and
possibly disastrous
locking together of two or
more genital piercings.

Clippesby *n.*
The errant fingernail you spy amongst
the coins from your pocket when offering
change in your upturned palm to the sub-
postmistress.

Cloghogle *v.*
To stare aghast at a bit of food stuck in
someone's teeth as they talk.

Clonbunny *n.*
One who 'doesn't smoke' but is still pinching
everybody else's.

Clontumpher *n.*
The pad on the forefinger used for tapping in
the last jigsaw piece.

Clovelly *adj.*
Quite nice, but not quite nice enough.

Clovulin *n.*
Protein extracted from four-leafed clovers and
sold in health food shops as 'concentrated luck'.

Clun *adj.*
Feeling down in the dumps when you get
home from a club.

Clunbury *n.*
The US Secret Service codename for the First
Lady's private parts.

Clyst Honiton *n.*
Weird guy you wouldn't look at twice if he
weren't a software billionaire.

Cobnash *n.*
Anything that falls out of your sandwich and
into your drink.

Cockadilly *adj.*
Momentarily taken aback by your own
reflection.

Cockermouth *n.*
A particularly offensive foul inside a rugby
scrum.

[34]

Cocking Causeway *n.*
A line of male spectators drinking on the
edge of a dance floor.

Cocumont *n.*
Any word invented by Shakespeare.

Colston Bassett *n.*
The widget concealed by
manufacturers inside washing machines
and dryers to make a quiet
clinking sound.

Compton Pauncefoot *n.*
One who
really
knows his
Flemish miniaturists.

Coptiviney *n.*
Large body of traffic cautiously trailing
behind what looks like a police car but
is actually a Highways Agency van.

Corippo *n.*
Badass pistachio nut that will tear your
nail off if you try to open it.

Corlattylannan *n.*
The bizarre name found on a personalised
mug in a souvenir shop in the course of
a fruitless search for Colin, Carol, Alan,
Anthony or Ann.

Corpusty *n.*
The mesmerising frond of dried matter that
goes in and out of a person's nose as they
breathe.

Corregidor *n.*
One who idly opens a fridge, stares gloomily
at the contents for a few seconds and then
shuts it again.

Cottered *adj.*
Whacked over the head without warning by a
rattle-wielding baby.

Cowhythe *n.*
Ancient item of farming equipment now only
used as a weapon in low-budget horror movies.

Cradley *n.*
A hat with ears on.

Creevins *pl.n.*
The imaginary substances that cling to your
palm after shaking hands with an undertaker.

Cricklade *n.*
The 'secret question' that fails to help you
remember a password.

Cricklewood *n.*
What ice-lolly sticks are made of.

Crigglestone *n.*
The invisible piece of grit on the sole of your
shoe designed to scratch other people's new
wooden floors.

Crimby *n.*
The transparently fake saunter of one who is
about to be stopped going through 'Nothing to
Declare'.

Crimcrest *n.*
The edge of a pie crust; the corrugation on a shin from a sock; the indentation on an arm gripped by a companion on a roller coaster.

Crindle *v.*
To fiddle unconsciously with one's hair.

Croome *v.*
To lock eyes with someone inside a parked car in the process of checking out your appearance in their window.

Croth *n.*
A shop that's had a 'Closing Down All Stock Must Go' sign for as long as you can remember.

Crotone *n.*
The small dry area on the corner of a damp towel.

Crowle *n.*
The fold in a double chin.

Cruft *n.*
Building originally intended for animals that now houses people.

Cruggion *n.*
The accumulation of crumbs, broken bits and shreds of plastic wrapper in the bottom of a biscuit tin.

Cruntully *adj.*
Deflated by watching a film on TV that's nowhere near as good as you remember it

Crunwear *n.*
Clothes you have for when no one is looking.

Cumberland *n.*
The part of a wet ploughed field that clings to your wellingtons and makes them look like clown shoes.

Cumberworth *n.*
One who complains before even being asked to do anything.

Cumledge *n.*
The place in the mind of a bigot where the second-hand and poisonous opinions are stored.

Curbans *pl.n.*
Towels wrapped round women's heads after washing their hair.

Curry Rivel *n.*
Something on the menu thoughtfully provided for those who've come to the wrong place: an omelette in an Indian restaurant; a pizza in a Greek restaurant; a vegetable in an Argentine restaurant.

Cutsyke *v.*
To pull every knife out of the block in search of the bread knife.

D

Daggons *pl.n.*
The thick-rimmed glasses worn by
management gurus.

Danby Wiske *n.*
The piece of kitchen equipment you never
use which makes the drawer impossible to
shut.

Dar es Salaam *n.*
The discarded end of a cured sausage with
the string still on.

Dargies *pl.n.*
People who reply at length and in detail to
the question 'How are you?'

Datchet *n.*
A small jacket worn by dachshunds in the
rain.

Davidson's Mains *pl.n.*
Terrible jokes that get big laughs when the
boss makes them.

Debach *v.*
To disengage gracefully from a cello.

Derrynacaheragh *n.*
Angry note left on a car windscreen informing
the driver they'll be killed if they park there
again.

Derryrush *n.*
The panic brought on by encountering a
police officer buying lunch in your local
corner shop.

Devizes *pl.n.*
The low-value coins
dropped in a public
place you're too lazy or
embarrassed to pick up.

Dibden Purlieu *n.*
A walk meant to last
'about four hours' that takes so long you end
up eating human flesh.

Didcot Parkway *n.*
An extended period of struggle in which one fails to grasp something: the opposite of a flash or revelation. 'Einstein stared at the problem for ten years. Then he saw it in a didcot parkway, rapidly swivelling his head from side to side as if trying to catch the name of a station from a passing train'. Steven Pinker, *How The Brain Turns To Porridge Sometimes*

Diggle *n.*
The little dance you do to make your underpants fit properly.

Dingle *n.*
A premonition that your phone is about to ring, just before it does.

Dinkelhausen *pl.n.*
The sort of dwellings depicted on Christmas cards.

Dolving *ptcpl.v.*
Circling a bonfire in a vain attempt to keep the smoke out of your eyes.

Doncaster *n.*
One who carries on the
conversation long after you've left
the room.

Dongolocking *ptcpl.v.*
Going in on the wrong side
for a kiss and bumping noses.

Donibristle *n.*
The bit you missed when shaving: a mauritius
(q.v.), for example.

Dorking *ptcpl.v.*
Doing work in an office that you know is of
absolutely no benefit to anyone but which
they're willing to pay you for anyway.

Dorney *adj.*
Unsure if you're awake enough to get up.

Dover *n.*
An ex-diver.

Drewton *n.*
The child in the school photograph with its
eyes closed.

Drimmo *n.*
One who looks like an off-duty superhero if he puts glasses on.

Drongan *n.*
An encrustation on the wall of a cheap hotel room that looks suspiciously like dried snot.

Dropmore *n.*
The illusion of rapid weight gain when sitting in a bath as it empties.

Drumnadrochit *n.*
The muffled snort of exasperation of one whose membership has recently expired.

Dublin *n.*
An unnecessary repetition of an already unnecessary phrase, as in 'at all, at all'.

Duckend Green *n.*
Lone vegetarian at a table of carnivores.

Dundry *adj.*
Described as 'phallic' but not resembling a penis – e.g. a tower block, a sports

car or a rifle.

Dungiven *adj.*
Gone but not forgiven.

Dunning *ptcpl.v.*
Happily reading a book in the loo.

Dunoon *v.*
To inveigle someone into a game you know
they cannot play.

Dunrossness *n.*
The feeling you've watched too many
episodes of *Friends* in a row.

Dunstable *n.*
A retired police officer.

DUNWEAR ¾   **Dunwear** *n.*
Beige clothing worn by old
people because they've seen
it on other old people.

Dutson *n.*
The hat worn in the Old West by the idiot
riding a donkey.

E

Eakring *n.*
A token of undying thrift.

East Anglia *n.*
When visiting a second-hand car auction and looking at two old Fords, this is the one on the right.

Ebberston *n.*
The latter part of the holiday, when time seems to speed up.

Ebford *n.*
Long-handled wooden rake used to push model tanks around in a war room.

Eccup *n.*
The mug that nobody uses because Grandad once kept his false teeth in it.

Egremont *n.*
Naff business that has tried to transform its image by adding an 'e' to the front – as in eplasticgnomes.co.uk.

Enderby *n.*
A parent absorbed in the stools of its offspring.

Erquery *n.*
Collection of instruction manuals for electrical equipment you've forgotten you ever owned.

Espelette *n.*
A paragraph you can't seem to take in no matter how many times you read it.

Esquerchin *n.*
One who enters a deserted gift shop, says hello to the hopeful owner, realises there

is nothing of interest for sale and leaves immediately.

Etting *ptcpl.v.*
Struggling to remember in the middle of an anecdote why you started telling it.

Evercreech *n.*
The sensation of toenails on nylon sheets.

Ewloe *n.*
The satisfying trickle of warm water out of your ear and onto the pillow the night after swimming.

Eworthy *adj.*
Of a person: worth emailing but not worth phoning or meeting.

Exmoor *n.*
A moor you've gone right off.

Eyeworth *n.*
An attractive fellow passenger reflected in the window.

F

Faccombe *v.*
To decide against helping those less fortunate
than yourself.

Farleaze *v.*
To sneeze so violently that the
papers on a colleague's desk are
disarranged.

Farthinghoe *n.*
A carefree little
laugh after breaking
wind in Pilates.

Fentral *adj.*
A long way from anywhere: in estate
agents' parlance, Peterborough and
King's Lynn are both in 'fentral London'.

Ferring *ptcpl.v.*
Performing a task in silence to show you don't agree with it.

Ffridd Faldwyn *n.*
A follower of the immemorial faith that you cannot get drunk if you only drink spritzers.

Fifield Bavant *n.*
A person whose only claim to fame is they know lots of famous people.

Fimber *v.*
To make yourself look good at crosswords by not admitting you did this one earlier today.

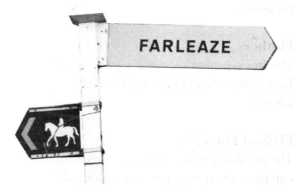

Fingal's Cave *n.*
The inevitable result of cheap lavatory paper.

Fiskerton *n.*
One who would wear a tie even if confined to bed.

Flappit Spring *n.*
A fancy-dress costume no one can identify.

Flashader *n.*
Small reflective object that lies on the ground trying to look like a contact lens.

Fletching *ptcpl.v.*
Storing up an erotic image for masturbatory purposes.

Flothers *pl.n.*
The frock-coated servants who agitate Sir Elton John's bubble bath with golden egg whisks.

Flyford Flavell *n.*
The jet of scalding coffee that surges from a cafetière when zealously over-plunged.

Folkestone *n.*
A hand-painted pebble from a seaside
souvenir shop.

Fomperron *n.*
The red bobble on top of a French sailor's hat.

Foscot *n.*
A sleeveless puffa jacket worn at country
fairs by loud people from Fulham.

Fowey *adj.*
Filled with self-loathing and despair after six
hours surfing the internet.

Framingham Pigot *n.*
A tap on the outside wall of a house that has
never worked.

Frampton-on-Severn *n.*
The group of late-night diners the staff wish
would bloody well finish their singing and go
home.

Frasseto *n.*
The tiny little hole in the perspex of an
aeroplane window.

Freuchies *pl.n.*
People who stand on the wrong side of the escalator.

Frinkle Green *n.*
Something frilly left on the side of the plate at Christmas lunch, because you're not sure if it's parsley or a bit of decoration from the ceiling.

Frisby on the Wreake *intcrj.*
Warning cry in a nudist colony.

Friskney *n.*
A saucy email exchange with a total stranger.

Fritton *n.*
In a bag of chips, the one with the eye.

Frobost *n.*
University official responsible for selecting the students on the front of the prospectus.

Frognal *n.*
A phone that stops ringing just as you get to it.

Frome *v.*
To peer through the slats of a Venetian blind.

Froncles *pl.n.*
The bumps on a Lincoln biscuit.

Fruence *n.*
The unique aroma of a foreign country.

Fryerning *ptcpl.v.*
Making brown marks on your clothes with an iron.

Fugglestone St Peter *n.*
The little pointy tool set into the cap of a tube of paste or ointment to enable you to break the seal.

Furneux Pelham *n.*
A suavely charming man who never fails to apologise for coming out without his wallet.

Furzey Lodge *n.*
A café that looks like someone's front room.

Fylingdales *pl.n.*
An adolescent male's first attempt at
sideburns.

G

Gailey Wharf *v.*
To begin running lightly up a flight of steps
to mask the fact that you've just tripped over
one.

Galaplan *n.*
Famous chess opening where White irritates
Black into making a mistake by continually
referring to the knights as 'horsies'.

Garmelow *n.*
The longed-for silence that follows a car
alarm.

Garstang *n.*
The smell of fish from an unexpected source.

Gawcott *n.*
A baby so ugly you can't even tell which way
up it is.

Gdansk *interj.*
What they say in Poland when you sneeze.

Geddington *n.*
A piece of A4 on which
three or four words have
been written and then
crossed out.

Gelligroes *pl.n.*
The strenuous facial
contortions of a man who is
shaving or watching the football.

Gerrots *n.*
The discarded ends of chopped root
vegetables.

Gerzat *n.*
A taxi driver's growled opinion that demands
your feeble assent.

Geurie *n.*
Admiring noise made by first-time parents
peering at an ultrasound scan in which
there's nothing discernibly human.

Gillygooly *adj.*
Anxious, nostalgic and relieved all at once as
you walk past your old school.

Glims Holm *n.*
The light left on by the occupant of a
glounthaune (q.v.) to lure people to their
doom.

Gloucester *n.*
The deflated skin bag of a popped blister.

Glounthaune *n.*
A lonely farmhouse at night.

Glutton Bridge *n.*
One of the few sexual positions attainable by
the morbidly obese.

Godalming *ptcpl.v.*
Spinning the batteries in the remote to
magically bring them back to life.

Goltho *n.*
The deformed but fanatically loyal servant of
a mad scientist.

Gomersal *n.*
A botched attempt to say goodbye to someone in the street before awkwardly heading off in the same direction.

Goodrich *n.*
One who gives to charity for tax reasons.

Goodworth Clatford *n.*
A neighbour or colleague you violently dislike in spite of the fact that they're clearly very nice.

Gorbals *n.*
The unheeded repetitive advice given by talkative self-service checkouts.

Gradgery *n.*
The insistence by elderly ladies who have fallen asleep in their armchairs that they were never asleep in the first place.

Grampound *v.*
To underestimate the weight differential between cooked and fresh spinach and make three people go hungry.

Grangebellew *n.*
The collective noun for parents at a public school rugby match.

Grantham *n.*
One who sniffs fruit in a supermarket.

Grassy Cletts *pl.n.*
The green streaks on a pair of cricketing trousers.

Grayshott *n.*
The litter of leaflets aimed at the over-sixties that falls out of the Sunday papers.

Greinton *n.*
An unexpected piece of sticking plaster found in your sock.

Gribbio *n.*
In Italian *commedia dell'arte*, the clown who
becomes prime minister.

Grishipoll *n.*
What Sean Connery had to climb to achieve
his success.

Gruting *ptcpl.v.*
Surreptitiously trying to remove a pubic hair
from your teeth.

Guilden Sutton *n.*
The sort of person who goes 'Aaahhh' when
sinking into an armchair.

Guith *adj.*
Magnetically evil and cunning, in the manner
of Guy of Gisborne.

Gurnard *n.*
Any small boy whose main skill seems to be
pulling faces.

Gussage All Saints *n.*
The curses and contortions of a woman peeing
in the woods as she tries to avoid her shoes or
a huish (q.v.).

Gussage St Michael *n.*
System used by Marks & Spencer's store
planners to ensure that the way to Men's
Socks always passes through Ladies'
Lingerie.

Gwennap *n.*
The disembodied voice in the lift.

H

H

Hackenthorpe *n.*
The clutch of smokers huddling outside a
public building in winter.

Hackforth *n.*
The disapproving pretend cough a non-
smoker produces in the vicinity of smokers.

Haigh *n.*
Informal greeting between horses.

Halamanning *ptcpl.v.*
Trembling violently, in the manner of a
washing machine at the end of its cycle.

Hallon *n.*
One who sometimes says hi and other times
ignores you.

Hampole *n.*
A fence post used to display a child's dropped glove.

Hampstead *n.*
The large ornamental knob at the bottom of the banisters that stopped Edwardian children sliding off the end to their deaths.

Hanbury *n.*
A family board game that's never been played because the rules are too complicated.

Hanging Grimston *n.*
The undercarriage of a toddler's nappy after ten hours' sleep plus breakfast.

Hanging Langford *n.*
Television term for the epoch that elapses between the words 'And the winner is . . .' and the actual announcement of the winner's name.

Hankerton *n.*
One who feels it is necessary to draw others' attention to the contents of their hanky.

Harburn *n.*
The intense, pained expression on a singer-songwriter's face before they start to sing.

Harpenden *n.*
The awkward silence after one person finishes making a complaint to another.

Hartley Mauditt *n.*
A tombstone in a Victorian cemetery, spattered with very old birdshit.

Haselbury Plucknett *n.*
The guff on the packaging of upmarket foods in which the makers declare how 'passionate' they are about cheese twirls.

Hassocks *interj.*
A mild expletive for ladies, when 'Botheration!' won't quite do.

Hastings *pl.n.*
Things left behind after leaving in a rush.

Hatfield *n.*
The sensation that one is still wearing a baseball cap long after it has been removed.

Hay-on-Wye *n.*
The classic New York vegetarian sandwich.

Hebden Bridge *n.*
The noise of a speaker fumbling for an acceptable alternative to the politically incorrect term they were on the point of uttering.

Heckmondwike *v.*
To frighten the life out of someone by accident.

Heddle *v.*
To ease off one gumboot with the heel of the other.

Heddon *n.*
One who continually assures you on a country walk that the car is just over the next hill.

Heglibister *n.*
A TV commercial so shouty it seems to be targeted at the people next door.

Hemel Hempstead *n.*
The unsynchronised mumble of a congregation at prayer.

Henglers *pl.n.*
Fishermen who only do it to get away from their wives.

Henlow *n.*
The crow of a cock that really isn't in the mood.

Henty *adj.*
Irritatingly chirpy in the face of a really serious situation.

[71]

Herning *ptcpl.v.*
Shifting anxiously from one leg to the other
while waiting for a credit-card transaction to
be processed.

Herserange *v.*
To scan the obituaries page for people you
know.

High Ireby *n.*
The state of being so angry about something
that you don't want what's making you angry
to stop.

Himbleton *n.*
The modicum of praise due to a man for
performing a domestic task.

Hinton Ampner *n.*
One who could have helped overhearing who
says 'I couldn't help overhearing'.

Hinton Waldrist *n.*
One who persistently returns to a subject no
one else is interested in.

Hobbister *n.*
The manky rug next to the cash machine with a dog on it.

Hoff *v.*
Of actors, to indicate deep emotion by looking up and to the right.

Honeybugle *v.*
To blow one's nose like a trumpet.

Hong *n.*
The slimiest of any given collection of dim sum.

Hoo Hole *n.*
The uncomfortable pause that follows phoning somebody and completely forgetting who it is you've called.

Horning *ptcpl.v.*
Trying to establish, without asking directly, if a person you fancy is attached.

Horse of Copinsay *n.*
Giant squiggle scratched on a chalk hillside that doesn't look remotely like a horse.

Hosta *n.*
Dried pasta in the bottom of the pan,
removable only by chisel.

Hreppholar *adj.*
Americans suffering from hreppholar disorder
are unable to pronounce the 'h' on the front of
'herb'.

Hüffelsheim *n.*
The joy of discovering your ex's new partner
is fatter than you.

Hüffenhardt *n.*
The little stab you get when you hear your ex
has a new partner, even though it was you that
did the dumping.

Hugus *n.*
One who, by the power of his atheistic
writings, achieves the status of a god.

Huish *n.*
The light brushing of wind, plant or insect
against the bare bottom of a woman crouching
for a Gussage All Saints (q.v.) in the woods.

Huish Champflower *n.*
A magnificently ornate American name, along
the lines of Lightbrush P. Bottomcrouch III.

Humbug Scrub *n.*
A cursory shower taken after an
act of
adultery.

Humptulips *pl.n.*
Scented gloves worn by drug mules to
search their own faeces.

Huney *n.*
A lifer's boyfriend.

Hungladder *adj.*
In a better mood as a result of discovering
there are lots of Germans around (usually
only experienced by another German).

Hurlet *n.*
A tiny child throwing stones into the sea and
missing.

Husbands Bosworth *n.*
Deliberately shoddy performance of a simple
domestic task by a man, so that he will never
be asked to do it again.

I

Illies *pl.n.*
People who scour the internet for new
diseases they might be suffering from.

Inchmahome *n.*
The long-drawn-out business of trying to get a
drunk onto a bus.

Ingleby Greenhow *n.*
An apprentice white plastic garden chair
designer.

Ings *pl.n.*
Things that don't start, won't start or haven't
started yet.

Inverarish *adj.*
Immune to being tickled.

Inverlune *v.*
To glare at the morons who applaud any
silence in a symphony.

Inverness *n.*
The loneliness of garden chairs in winter.

Inworth *n.*
One who puts their face too close to you when
they talk.

Isbister *n.*
One who nods sagely while you're talking, to
indicate they already know what you're about
to say.

J

Jackadgery *n.*
The irritating hiss from the headphones of the
person next to you.

Jamberoo *n.*
Festival wristband worn as a souvenir.

Jeffcott *n.*
The imaginary tool left behind by workmen
that enables them to get back in their van and
go away again almost as soon as they arrive.

Jilakin *n.*
The warm smile from the girl behind the
counter that suggests you're special.

Jimboomba *n.*
A cushion placed
inside a bass drum.

Johnby *n.*
A person who uses your name too much when they're talking to you, John.

K

Kadnook *n.*
The drawer where your mother keeps all the
presents you gave her that she never liked.

Kangarilla *n.*
The interestingly complicated stalk left after
eating a bunch of grapes.

Kangy Angy *adj.*
Distressed and
disoriented by the
supermarket having
inexplicably moved
things around.

Kanumbra *n.*
The sense that someone is
standing behind you.

Keetmanshoop *n.*
A loop on a pair of trousers that was missed when the belt was put on.

Keith Inch *n.*
(MEASURE) The amount of *In Our Time* the average person understands.

Kenmare *n.*
The guy in a nightclub who seemed like a good idea until he opened his mouth.

Kennythorpe *n.*
Cheeky-chappy street dance used in musicals to portray Cockneys.

Kettletoft *n.*
The bits of hair and blood on a riot policeman's truncheon.

Kewstoke *v.*
To interrupt a yawn or stretch by poking someone in the ribs.

Kiel Crofts *pl.n.*
Lunatic tufts of hair that denote genius in the possessor.

Kilkeary *adj.*
Convinced by a scary article that you have
a tropical disease, even though you've never
left Buckinghamshire.

Killiecrankie *n.*
A look warning someone to shut up before
they've said anything.

Killinardrish *n.*
The sound of a cutlery basket falling to the
floor.

Killybegs *pl.n.*
The cries by which a baby signifies that it no
longer wishes to be tickled.

Kilwinning *ptcpl.v.*
Savagely piercing the film on an oven-ready
carton in the manner of a slasher-movie
villain.

Kingledoors *pl.n.*
The monogrammed flaps on cardboard boxes
owned by the Royal Family.

King's Newton *n.*
The greatest book you've ever bought but
never actually read.

King's Pyon *n.*
A chess move where all the pieces are swept
from the board prior to running up to one's
bedroom in tears.

Kirby-le-Soken *n.*
Someone who hasn't used the dryer in
the lavatory properly and emerges to find
themselves obliged to shake hands.

Kirk Smeaton *n.*
A teenager proud of having acquired his
sexually transmitted disease.

Kirkbuddo *n.*
Expendable minor character destined to die
in the first fifteen minutes of the film.

Kirkwhelpington *n.*
The noise and associated one-legged dance
produced by standing on a Lego brick in bare
feet.

Kirtling *ptcpl.v.*
Benign kettling, such as that required to keep a small child moving in the right direction.

Kittitoe *v.*
To step delicately around a small blob of gunk ejected by a cat which you have no intention of helping to mop up.

Klemzig *n.*
One who is sexually aroused by the thought of a rabbi.

The Knab *n.*
Nickname by which an irritating male colleague refers to himself: 'What a night! The Knab is seriously tired today, guys!'

Knill *n.*
The white curd that oozes out of budget bacon.

Knockandhu *n.*
Fear brought on by the words 'Don't take this personally but . . .'

Koolyanobbing *ptcpl.v.*
Feeling a pregnant woman's bump without
asking first.

Krumlin *n.*
The centre of power of any crap organisation.

Kuala Lumpur *n.*
A cuddly toy hideously disfigured by the
sexual attentions of a dog.

Kyle Lodge *n.*
Any objection to a planning application based
purely on spite.

L

Lancaster *n.*
One who enacts spells over long distances.

Largs *pl.n.*
The improbable number of crumbs that fall out of a toaster when you move it.

Lechlade *v.*
To coat one's beloved in cottage cheese.

Leoh *n.*
A little gasp from being hugged too tightly.

Letchworth *n.*
The door charge at a lap-dancing club.

Letheringsett *n.*
Elderly German couple commencing their fifteenth week on a Lanzarote nudist beach.

Levitt Hagg *interj.*
What Ray Winstone says when he's not in the mood.

Lewisham *n.*
The brief moment of panic between realising your car keys aren't in your pocket and remembering that's because you're driving.

Licola *n.*
The girl in the sixth form who has an entourage.

Lispopple *n.*
A completed item added to a To Do list, purely for the satisfaction of instantly crossing it off again.

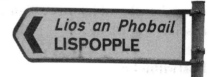

Little Kelk *n.*
The infant in the photo on your desk who's now twenty-nine.

Little Stukeley *n.*
A small boy running round a park pretending to be an aeroplane.

Lizard Siding *ptcpl.v.*
Taking a circuitous route to avoid charity
muggers and *Big Issue* vendors.

Ljubljana *interj.*
What people say to the dentist on the way out.

Llandrillo *n.*
One who swaggers about in a toolbelt.

Loughedge *n.*
The sort of person who spells 'phone or 'plane
with an apostrophe.

Lostock Junction *n.*
The point after which you will drink
absolutely anything.

Lostwithiel *n.*
The feeling that you have no idea where you
are, but nor does anyone else.

Loudwater *n.*
A child's strongly held opinion, copied word
for word from its parents.

Loughborough *n.*
The false gusto with which children eat vegetables in adverts.

Love Clough *n.*
Any orifice unexpectedly explored during sex.

Low Etherley *n.*
The melancholy feeling of immense sorrow and wisdom caused by looking at the night sky after too much wine.

Low Snaygill *n.*
One who combs the internet looking for spelling mistakes.

Low Whinnow *n.*
Opening section of 'Thought for the Day', intended to lull the audience into the false belief that the subject of religion isn't about to come up.

Lower Sheering *ptcpl.v.*
Publicly disengaging a wedgie.

Lulworth Cove *n.*
The man in the cinema who goes 'shush'.

Lunning *ptcpl.v.*
Hovering on the edge of a circle of people you
don't know.

Lydiard Millicent *n.*
In the novels of Jane Austen, any character
who is mentioned but has no dialogue.

M

Macerata *pl.n.*
Miraculous red marks on the knuckles,
caused by an encounter with a) the Virgin
Mary or b) a nutmeg grater.

McGregor's Corner *n.*
The part of a Scottish pub from which the
locals glare at strangers.

Macroom *v.*
Of an electric kettle, to go on enthusiastically
boiling long after it should have switched
itself off.

Maesog *n.*
The feeling of having stepped in something
wet while wearing socks.

Maesycrugiau *n.*
The unaccountable slight increase in weight
experienced by dieters.

Malahide *v.*
To conceal oneself so successfully during a game of hide-and-seek that everyone gives up and goes home.

Malmö *adj.*
Happily tired.

Manaus *adj.*
Slightly flat and confused, as when finishing what you thought was a really good book, only to discover that no one on Amazon has given it more than one star.

Manjimup *n.*
A prisoner who tries to start a Mexican wave in solitary confinement.

Manningtree *n.*
Family member obsessed with genealogy who regularly emails with news of third cousins twice removed in New Zealand.

Marganure *v.*
To emboss the manufacturer's name on a manhole cover.

Martin Hussingtree *n.*
The kid in your year who used a briefcase.

Mastrils *pl.n.*
Alarming or unconventional pets such as
ferrets or anacondas.

Mauritius *n.*
The clump of pubic hair that always gets
missed when one is shaving one's scrotum.

Meathop *n.*
Close encounter with a rock star in a flight
departure lounge, which you will remember
all your life and they don't even register.

Meckering *ptcpl.v.*
Quietly carrying on with your emails while
pretending to listen to your mother on the
phone.

Meigle *v.*
To endlessly bring the conversation back to
oneself.

Melby *n.*
The thing you forgot to buy that was the
reason you went shopping in the first place.

Melcombe Horsey *n.*
The collective noun for Sloane Rangers
skiing with no trousers on and bras over their
sweaters.

Memel *v.*
To continue vaguely agreeing with someone
you stopped listening to ages ago.

Menadarva *n.*
A higher plane that can only be reached by
wearing the right training shoes.

Menangle *v.*
To shift position in your seat to get a better
view of an eyeworth (q.v.).

Meon *n.*
A book you buy for your partner and end up
reading yourself.

Metricup *n.*
The amount of mucus in a giant's
handkerchief.

Mevagissey *adj.*
Stupefied by a display of Christmas lights on
a suburban house that makes it look like a
state-owned fairground in Hong Kong.

Micheldever *n.*
The tool they use on golf courses to make the
holes.

Michigan *n.*
A problem that
manifests itself only
when nobody else is
present.

Middlezoy *n.*
That part of a zoy which is at
neither end.

Midsomer Norton *n.*
A village cricket match disturbed by a
vintage motorcycle.

Mill Craig *n.*
Picturesque derelict shack on the seashore entirely surrounded by watercolour artists.

Millom *n.*
The dénouement of a movie after the audience has guessed the end.

Milverton *n.*
Any notebook that's completely blank – apart from the first page which reads: 'Thoughts and Ideas: 2007'.

Minsk *n.*
Something that looks like ground beef but
isn't.

Minskip *n.*
The smallest of the imperial units of volume,
now only used for the fruit juice glasses on
hotel breakfast buffets.

Minterburn *n.*
Agonising rise in the temperature of your
shower, because someone has turned on a
cold tap elsewhere in the house.

Mirkady Point *n.*
The precise time in the middle of the night
when oligarchs and actors have to get up to
shave, so their stubble looks just right in the
morning.

Miskin *n.*
Expensively dressed thin woman who goes on
about how fat she is.

Mittagong *n.*
The glove worn by percussionists to mute
cymbals.

Mockerkin *n.*
Rain dance performed by people trying to put
waterproof trousers on.

Molepolole *n.*
One who calls out catchphrases to comedians
in the street.

Monzambano *n.*
A hotel bathroom so small you can't get
through the door without climbing over the
lavatory.

Morfa *n.*
New texting acronym you can't work out,
though you're pretty sure what the 'f' stands
for.

Morpeth *n.*
Vague feeling of regret you get when you hear
of the death of someone you had no idea was
still alive.

Mountnessing *ptcpl.v.*
Sitting on your boyfriend's shoulders at a
festival and waving your arms from side to
side.

Moy *n.*
A small wart absent-mindedly toyed with by
its owner.

Much Wenlock *n.*
The point in a relationship when she
continually brings up the subject of marriage.

Muchlarrick *n.*
The implausible joy caused by the acquisition
of a new sofa in a television commercial.

Muckle Skerry *n.*
The mess you've stopped noticing because it's
become so familiar.

Muker *n.*
One who retches slightly when using a spoon
to clean the back of their tongue.

Mungo Brush *n.*
A kiss between two bearded men.

Munising *ptcpl.v.*
Sizing up what the shopper ahead of you in
the supermarket queue has bought.

Murist *n.*
A creator of felt-tip pen cock-and-balls art.

Murroes *pl.n.*
The tramlines made by dragging a fork across
mashed potato.

N

Naddle *v.*
To juggle, entangle or bestrew recalcitrant coat hangers.

Nantwich *n.*
A snack where the filling drops out, leaving an empty husk.

Narridy *adj.*
Nervous of triggering the airport metal detector.

Nedging *ptcpl.v.*
Shuffling your suitcase along to close the gap in an airport queue.

Neen Savage *n.*
An angry glare at an inanimate object you have just bumped into.

Nelling *ptcpl.v.*
Incessantly trying on clothes.

Nelsherry *n.*
One who rummages furiously in her handbag.

Ness of Tenston *n.*
The winding handle on a tennis net.

Nether Button *n.*
That which, if touched, is guaranteed to make someone really angry.

Nether Stowey *n.*
Illegal drug, transported anally and extracted with humptulips (q.v.).

Netheravon *n.*
Any nook, cranny or cavity with enough room for either a small object or your fingertips – but not both – to get into.

Newton Mearns *n.*
An awareness that apples are falling nearby.

Newton Poppleford *n.*
Person at a Q & A who asks a question which
turns out not to be a question at all, merely a
long, convoluted and pompous statement of
their own very important opinion.

Newtonmore *n.*
One who stands on the shoulders of giants in
order to pee further.

Nibun *n.*
Half a tennis ball, painted green and pink to
look like a pudding, put on the conveyor belt
by the staff in a Japanese restaurant as a joke.

Niederbipp *n.*
A small child who hits you when you turn
your back.

Noards *pl.n.*
The bits of wall behind radiators that never
get painted.

Norristhorpe *n.*
The first person in a motorway traffic jam to
get out of their car and walk about sighing.

North Piddle *n.*
Stream of outdoor urine redirected by the wind.

Nouster *n.*
One who is so clever you can't understand a word they're saying.

Nudgee *n.*
Beneficiary in a will who inherits the deceased's Tesco Bag for Life.

Nunkeeling *ptcpl.v.*
Bending to determine the eyeline between one's body parts and the windowsill, to see what might have been on view to the neighbours after getting changed with the curtains open.

Nunney *n.*
Comforting wad of folded paper in the pocket that turns out to be old receipts and napkins when offered as money.

Nurney *adj.*
The way a person's face looks when they've
just said 'I told you so'.

Nutgrove *n.*
The place provided by a newspaper for
readers to comment online.

Nymet Tracey *n.*
A beard that follows the jawline and looks
like it's been glued on.

O

Oakhanger *n.*
(ARCHAIC) One who spent his or her
childhood climbing trees.

Obergurgl *n.*
A dinner-party guest who finds
it amusing to spill red wine on
his chinos and spend the rest of
the evening claiming he's been
shot.

Ogdens *pl.n.*
Privacy-protecting designer
dark glasses worn indoors at
night, which make celebrities
immediately identifiable.

Old Edlington *n.*
Someone who greets you with discomfiting
warmth, having apparently forgotten how
much you hated each other at school.

Omdurman *n.*
One who mumbles incoherently while dozing
in a chair.

Oodnadatta *n.*
Pattern of small holes in a teenager's bedroom
wall, visible only when the drawing pins are
removed and the posters are taken down.

Ormskirk *n.*
A person you're not sure whether to tip.

Osmotherley *adj.*
Reeking of perfume after a bosomy hug from
a middle-aged lady.

Oulton *n.*
A person you get on with perfectly well but
wouldn't want to socialise with.

Ouyen *n.*
Affirmative response to a dentist's question
mid-procedure.

Oving *ptcpl.v.*
Timidly tapping an egg against the rim of a
bowl so as not to crack it too much.

Oyster Skerries *pl.n.*
Those wire contraptions that look like part
of a lampshade, used in smart restaurants to
serve shellfish.

Ozleworth *n.*
The blissful aftermath of a sneeze.

P

Painswick *n.*
Forgettable art in hotel rooms; the visual equivalent of muzak.

Peakirk *n.*
One who regularly points out that there are no lavatories on the USS *Enterprise*.

Peatling Parva *n.*
A piece of cheese carefully put back in the fridge even though it's too small and dried up to be of any further use.

Peening Quarter *n.*
The final fifteen minutes spent in dreaded anticipation of a family gathering.

Pendomer *n.*
One who takes a pen from the pot, discovers it doesn't work and puts it back again.

Pennyvennie *n.*
A yummy mummy's yummy mummy.

Penton Mewsey *n.*
An innocuous-sounding question your partner asks you to which there is only one acceptable answer.

Penzance *n.*
(ARCHAIC) Permanent ink-stained dent on a fountain pen user's finger.

Pepper Arden Bottoms *pl.n.*
Shakespearean jokes where you feel obliged to join in the laughter, even though you've no idea what they mean.

Philadelphia *n.*
The sound of several magazines falling off the arm of a sofa.

Philippines *pl.n.*
Ladyboys formerly known as Philip.

Pinvin *n.*
Something you order online when drunk
and forget about till it arrives in a van to be
signed for.

Pipe and Lyde *n.*
A couple who are respectively 6'4" and
4'11".

Plaistow *n.*
A grudging agreement between two parties
that suits neither.

Plean *v.*
To half-heartedly wipe a café table.

Plenisette *n.*
A wisp of cellophane that sticks to your hand
no matter how hard you try to shake it off.

Plocrapool *n.*
The bin in a Greek hotel designed exclusively
for used lavatory paper.

Pluckanes *pl.n.*
The tiny little I-shaped plastic tags that snap off when you pull the labels from new clothes, then live in your carpet with the toenail clippings.

Pluckley *n.*
The feather stalk residue that remains on a frozen chicken.

Pockley *adj.*
Unsure, when describing a person, if you should mention the colour of their skin.

Pocklington *n.*
The pointy indentation in a jacket that has been left on a coat hook for too long.

The Pole of Itlaw *n.*
Remote and inaccessible part of a woman's body, now officially declared an erogenous zone. The Pole was not reached until 1974, after more than a century of unsuccessful expeditions. The 1911 Redvers-Harkin attempt ended in tragedy, when all four men died of exhaustion after several hours' fruitless searching in the dark.

Polegate *v.*
To delay giving an opinion until you know what will go down well.

Polyphant *n.*
One who knows many ways to ingratiate himself.

Pont-y-Pant *n.*
Alpha male brought down by fraud or inappropriate sex.

Pontypool *v.*
To put your pants on inside out, then take them off again and put them on the right way round.

Pootilla *n.*
A collection of toddlers on a floor, all ignoring each other.

Pootings *pl.n.*
Little snorts of derision that aren't meant to be heard but somehow always are.

Poplars *pl.n.*
Fun girls who turn their names into rhymes,
as when Isabel Wilson becomes Izz Wizz.

Poringland *n.*
That part of an Argos store where the
catalogues are located.

Portsoy *n.*
The mysterious ingredient in Marmite and
Simon Cowell that makes people love them or
hate them.

Potto *adj.*
Confused by the dish put in front of you,
because it doesn't look anything like the
description in the menu.

Poughkeepsie *n.*
One who supervises, curates or commentates
on another's colonic irrigation.

Powfoot *v.*
To come straight to the point with no regard
for tact or sensitivity; the opposite of
'pussyfoot'.

Poynings *pl.n.*
Festive items placed on
a gate to let revellers
know you're ready for
them.

Prayle Grove *n.*
The fear in the eyes of
a groom as the best man
stands up to speak.

Praze-an-Beeble *n.*
The pair of witty signs or symbols on adjacent
doors in a restaurant, which leaves you unsure
if you're entering the Ladies or the Gents.

Prestatyn *n.*
The little button on the lid of a jar that goes
pop if it hasn't been opened before.

Primrose Valley *n.*
A freshly washed lady garden.

Prisk *v.*
To size up a man by asking where his ski
chalet is and what kind of wife he drives.

Prospidnick *n.*
A pillow that appears to have doubled in size since it was last put into a pillowcase.

Prowse *v.*
To act cool after scoring a brilliant goal, as if you do it all the time.

Putton *n.*
A pointless button, such as the two or three on each cuff of a man's suit jacket.

Pyongyang *n.*
The noises made by little boys playing cops and robbers.

Q

Quadring Eaudike *n.*
A question such as 'Don't you like me?' to
which the answers 'Yes' and 'No' both sound
wrong.

Quambone *n.*
The part of an adolescent that makes them
feel they stick out.

Quarff *n.*
The tiny useless pocket above the real pocket
in a pair of jeans.

Quarles *pl.n.*
The voices women put on when they want
something.

Quarmby *n.*
Gruesome animal product considered a
delicacy in just one region.

Quatremare *n.*
Four women crying in unison.

Quatsino *n.*
Theoretical subatomic particle accounting
for the fact that articles about gay people
proliferate while their number remains
constant.

Quatt *n.*
An exotic new supermarket fruit, possibly
related to the zumpango (q.v.).

Queets *pl.n.*
The maddening bits of price label that can't
be scratched off; hence, those who stick
around when they're obviously not wanted.

Quernmore *n.*
An innocent-looking advertisement for
making money at home, which leads to you
faking orgasms down the phone.

Quetico *n.*
The tiny speech bubble that pops up when an
empty text is sent.

Quidnish *adj.*
Gifted with the power to recall the plot details
of each and every *Harry Potter* book and
movie.

Quilquox *n.*
Budget-conscious 'invisible ink' used by MI5:
messages are pressed into the paper with
biros that have run out.

Quinton *n.*
A man whose entire adult life was determined
by his first term at Eton.

R

Rackwallace *n.*
The awful realisation that the person you've been talking to all this time is not who you thought they were.

Ramna Stacks *pl.n.*
The little piles of children's books and shoes left at the bottom of the stairs for taking up later.

Ratagan *n.*
Ecologically sound floor covering made from recycled espadrilles.

Rathcrogue *n.*
A small girl who is all sweetness and light when adults are around, but a nasty little beast when they're not looking.

Remenham *n.*
The residue left on the wrapper of a peeled muffin.

Rhughasinish *n.*
Ancient gestural language used by Mongolian elk wranglers and bookies on a racecourse.

Rhydding *ptcpl.v.*
Nodding and smiling when you can't hear what someone's saying because of the music.

Rhyl *n.*
A used roll of film sitting in a drawer that's never been developed and is now never going to be.

Ribble *v.*
To manufacture, manoeuvre or steal
corrugated iron.

Rickmansworth *n.*
The percentage of a nation's GDP wasted on
gym membership.

Ringaskiddy *adj.*
So excited by good news that you bound up
the stairs two at a time.

Rishangles *pl.n.*
The blackened parts in the corners of an
otherwise gleaming silver roasting tin.

Rissington *n.*
A bar suspended from a kitchen ceiling
from which pans are hung. Hence Little
Rissington, Upper Rissington, Great
Rissington.

Rockness *n.*
The leathery exterior common to lizards and
members of the Rolling Stones.

Rooking *ptcpl.v.*
Going round the room after a party,
consuming all the leftover wine and crisps.

Ruddle *v.*
To mime quotation marks with your fingers.

Ruswarp *v.*
To deliberately write a word unclearly when
you don't know how to spell it.

S

St Serf's Inch *n.*
The amount by which coffin lids in the
Middle Ages were left ajar so that those
mistakenly buried alive could shout for help.

St Veep *n.*
The patron saint of mobiles that are lost while
switched to silent.

Salmon Gums *n.*
Unwanted mouth-to-mouth contact with an
elderly relative when an attempted kiss on
the cheek goes awry.

Salterhebble *v.*
To step in and out of the tyres on an obstacle
course.

Sand Hutton *n.*
A small jellyfish brought on a spade by
a child to a parent that turns out to be a
discarded condom.

Sargasso *n.*
One who thinks it's amusing to walk into a
second-hand bookshop and ask if they have
Fly Fishing by J. R. Hartley.

Scarasta *n.*
Constellation that will never be famous
because no one can agree on what it looks like.

Scatness *n.*
A child's feigned interest in the front of a
birthday card before opening it up to see how
much cash falls out.

Scatsta *n.*
The mark made by the striking of the first
match against a new box.

Schwentinental *adj.*
The all-purpose accent used by amateur
actors to play Germans, Turks, Czechs,
Scandinavians, Belgians and Greeks.

Scopus *n.*
Charity with an important-sounding name
that doesn't actually tell you who it helps.

Scratby *n.*
A dried-up felt-tip pen kept in the pot by the
phone.

Scremby *n.*
A pencil with a broken point kept in the pot
by the phone.

Scrivelsby *n.*
A chopstick, child's paintbrush, knitting
needle, screwdriver, drinking straw, Allen key
or pencil torch removed one after the other
from the pot by the phone in a frantic search
for a biro.

Scrooby *n.*
A biro that runs out halfway through taking
down a vital message.

Scudellate *adj.*
Shaped like the bit on the windscreen the
wipers never reach.

Sculms *pl.n.*
The clean-shaven areas of Hitler's top lip on
either side of his moustache.

Scunthorpe *v.*
To insert an
expletive into a
word for the sake
of emphasis, as in
'Fan-bloody-tastic!'

Scurdie Ness *n.*
Other people's
rubbish on a café
table you have to clear away before you can
sit down.

Seave Green *n.*
A person who'd quite like to save the planet
but is not all that bothered; an acquaintance
of the earth, rather than a friend.

Sentosa *n.*
The horror and alarm that strike when you
realise you have just hit 'Reply All' by
mistake.

Sepon *n.*
Something you buy for yourself after not
getting it for Christmas.

Sezincote *n.*
The little label with the dry-cleaning
instructions on.

Shackerstone *n.*
One who looks about them after walking into
a plate-glass window to see if anyone noticed.

Shap *n.*
Folded paper or card wedged in a window to
stop it rattling in the wind.

Shimpling *ptcpl.v.*
Vigorously pretending to be doing the thing
you should have been doing as soon as you
hear your partner's key in the front door.

Shooter's Hill *n.*
Legendary South London drama school,
where geezers teach the sons of geezers how
to play geezers.

Shunnies *pl.n.*
Footwear belonging to someone else, temporarily borrowed for the purpose of carrying the kitchen rubbish to the bin outside.

Silsden *n.*
The sediment found at the bottom of a mug after biscuit dunking.

Simister *n.*
A building that looks like something else, such as a gherkin or cheesegrater.

Simoda *n.*
The kind of car they haven't made for forty years but which is still seen in the West Country.

Sinton *n.*
Circular mark caused by placing a hot mug on a table.

Sittingbourne *n.*
The indentation in a well used armchair.

Skallary *n.*
Factory producing Scandinavian TV crime series.

Skares *pl.n.*
Individual eyebrow hairs.

Skeeby *n.*
One who leaves a tip and then hangs around to see what kind of reaction it gets.

Skeete *n.*
The sound made by players' shoes in an indoor sports arena.

Skeffling *ptcpl.v.*
The jiggling of potatoes in the roasting pan or the letter cubes in a Boggle grid.

Skelton *n.*
A door not attached to anything.

Skirling *ptcpl.v.*
Lulling someone into a false sense of security with small talk before you chuck, sack or behead them.

Slaithwaite *v.*
To keep one eye shut when having a pee in the middle of the night.

Slattocks *pl.n.*
All the numbers in a lottery that didn't come up.

Smailholm *n.*
A holiday postcard that arrives back home after you do.

Smeeth *v.*
To smile meekly at passport control.

Smoke Hole *n.*
The part of a CEO or VIP that is advantageous to blow into.

Snaith *n.*
Envy of another person's Twitter following.

Snaresbrook *n.*
An incriminating protestation of innocence
before being accused of anything, as when
a five-year-old appears downstairs to inform
you they didn't bite Nicola.

Solent Breezes *pl.n.*
Smooth assurances by architects that your
building will be completed on time; by
lawyers that you'll win your
case; and
by doctors
that there's
absolutely
nothing to worry
about.

Soppog *n.*
Lacklustre anal
intercourse.

Soroba *n.*
An African tribe so far-flung they haven't
heard of Stephen Fry.

Sorrento *n.*
The thing that goes round and round as a
YouTube video loads.

South Harting *ptcpl.v.*
Strategically concealing your private parts as
you change into your swimming costume on
the beach.

Southerndown *n.*
The first inkling that all is not well with the
socks in your wellington boots.

Spalding *ptcpl.v.*
The futile waving of the hand in front
of the mouth when eating something
much hotter
than expected.

Spath *n.*
Trail of takeaway debris on the street
from rubbish sacks attacked in the night
by creatures.

Spaxton *n.*
The lead commuter who is always
first off the train.

Spen *n.*
Pronged price marker stuck in delicatessen cheese.

Spittal of Glenmuick *n.*
An extreme case of salmon gums (q.v.).

Springboig *n.*
The mass sprint at the start of a school cross-country race, which none of the runners can sustain.

Sproatley *n.*
Perky centenarian who attributes his or her longevity to smoking sixty cigarettes a day.

Sproxton *n.*
One who feels no guilt about marching into a pub just to use the toilet.

Standish *adj.*
Approachable, warm, friendly; not standoffish.

Stanway *n.*
The path of a stairlift.

Stathe *n.*
The long boring bit of the Budget that's got nothing to do with booze.

Steg *n.*
The stain on the crotch of a man's trousers that he insists is food.

Sticklepath *n.*
A track in the woods that starts off promisingly but almost immediately ends in an impenetrable thicket.

Stirling *n.*
A very small teaspoon.

Stockleigh Pomeroy *n.*
The manhunt that takes place after a murder, to find a neighbour willing to say the line: 'He kept himself to himself.'

Stocklinch Magdalen *n.*
(RARE) The astonishment experienced on seeing the Virgin Mary twice in the same day.

Stocklinch Ottersey *n.*
The astonishment experienced on seeing a

word you've never come across before twice
in the same day. 'Stonganess', for example.

Stonganess *n.*
The feeling partway through a DVD box
set when it starts to be more like work than
pleasure.

Straidbilly *n.*
Someone behind you in a long queue.

Straidkilly *n.*
Someone ahead of you in a long queue.

Stranagalwilly *n.*
Attack of murderous rage when the last
straidkilly (q.v.) finally gets served and turns
out to be the slowest blithering idiot in the
universe.

Stranagappoge *n.*
The tangle of knotted wires anchoring plastic
toys to the packaging that's impossible to
undo.

Stranocum *n.*
The green pimple in the dimple of an orange.

[141]

Stratford Tony *n.*
The windbag in
the pub who
claims to know
'some pretty
heavy-duty
people down the
East End'.

Strawberry Bank *n.*
Unmanned café counter where they keep the
sugar, spoons and napkins.

Stroat *n.*
Any unidentified species of roadkill.

Strogue *v.*
To walk like a shoplifter.

Stromness *n.*
The euphoria that follows emerging from a
very cold sea.

Strood *n.*
Human droppings in a laptop keyboard,
such as dandruff, flakes of skin, skares (q.v.),
utrillas (q.v.) and clippesbys (q.v.).

Strubby with Woodthorpe *n.*
Comedy double act where you can't tell who's
meant to be the funny one.

Stubbington *n.*
One who refuses all invitations unless their
dog's conditions are met.

Studley Roger *n.*
A partner's alarming ex-boyfriend who seems
to possess every quality a girl could wish for
in a man.

Suishnish *adj.*
In a mood to pull back the curtains with a
flourish.

Sulham *n.*
The reproachful glare of the landline phone
you don't use any more.

Surrey *n.*
A mumbled and manifestly insincere apology
forced out of a six-year-old.

Sutton *n.*
A futon folded fat enough to be sat on.

Swaffham Bulbeck *n.*
The ballooning of swimwear caused by
stepping into slightly deeper water than
anticipated.

Swanbister *n.*
A character, such as Bridget Jones or
Columbo, whose lovable incompetent flapping
conceals a cool intelligence beneath.

Swaythling *ptcpl.v.*
Standing in the shop wondering whether to
buy the Fairtrade one or the one you actually
want.

Sweening *ptcpl.v*
Pouring liquid as slowly as possible into an
obviously too small container.

Swona *n.*
The collective glow of Apple logos from a
group of laptops.

Sychtyn *n.*
Anti-synchronous body language, such as
deliberately walking out of step with someone
you don't like.

[144]

Sydling St Nicholas *n.*
The last old rector in England to actually live
in an Old Rectory.

Symbister *n.*
A pair of lovers who look like brother and
sister.

T

Tahila *n.*
An all-purpose Spanish word used when attempting to remember the lyrics of 'Guantanamera'.

Tansley *adj.*
How one feels on the first day of autumn.

Tapnage *n.*
The hand-waving and peering under the washbasin required to get the water flowing in an overly stylish bathroom.

Tatlows Folly *n.*
A recipe containing two or more ingredients you've never heard of.

Teddington Lock *adj.*
A gaze from a stranger held a delicious mite too long.

Te'ekiu *n.*
A traditional tea ceremony. Having made
two identical cups of tea, and sensing one is
marginally better than the other, the teamaker
must decide which to keep.

Teesside *n.*
System of carrying two teacups into another
room with one in the right hand to remember
which was yours.

Teetz *n.*
The sheepish expression worn when
presenting a left-hand cup of tea, while
hoping that no one else uses this method of
tea delivery.

Teevurcher *n.*
One who glares suspiciously, under the
distinct impression they have just been
offered a substandard cup of tea.

Templeshambo *n.*
The act of ruining the day of all the financiers
in the room, last achieved by Jesus Christ
about two thousand years ago.

Termonfeckin *ptcpl.v.*
Unhelpfully pre-empting what a stutterer is
trying to say; hence the Google algorithm that
tells you what you aren't searching for.

Terryglass *n.*
The member of a band who leaves just before
it gets famous.

Theddlethorpe *n.*
Genital discomfort of a pantomime dame after
a vigorous ride on a pantomime horse.

Thil *n.*
The sprig of plastic tubing left behind after
using a wire stripper.

Thirroul *n.*
The bond that divides, the gulf that unites;
as with a couple sitting next to each other
separately absorbed in their laptops.

Thornton Heath *n.*
An alluring patch of grass that turns prickly
and stony as soon as a picnic rug is laid over
it.

Thornton Steward *n.*
One who answers his telephone by clearly
stating the number.

Thorpe Thewles *pl.n.*
The almost inaudible noises soap makes as it
slips out of your hand and you try and fail to
catch it again.

Thrashbush *n.*
(MEDICAL) The principal cause of
absenteeism amongst UK sex workers
between 1931 and 1967.

Throsk *n.*
A pubic hair that gets stuck in your
throat.

Thurning *ptcpl.v.*
Camply running round a dog show
alongside a dog.

Thurrock *v.*
To hunt frantically through the contents of a drawer while the taxi is waiting outside.

Thursby *n.*
One who remarks how quickly the week has gone.

Tidworth *n.*
The amount of drink in your glass when you ask for 'a very small one' and then are disappointed by how little you get.

Tildonk *n.*
The wedge-shaped plastic thing placed on a supermarket conveyor belt between one person's shopping and another's.

Timbo *n.*
An unexpired Pay and Display car-park ticket thoughtfully stuck on the Pay Here machine.

Timbold *adj.*
Very slightly and pointlessly brave, as in one who says 'boo' to a distant goose.

Tinkerbush *n.*
One who is addicted to bikini waxes.

Tipton *n.*
An imaginary doffing of the hat in silent acknowledgement of high-class work.

Tittybong *n.*
One who complains about women who breastfeed in public, but buys the *Sun* every day for Page 3.

Toames *n.*
The first furtive touching of toes in bed after a severe row with your partner.

Tobermory *n.*
The sound of a dog dreaming.

Todwick *n.*
A small frond of lavatory paper found sticking to the end of a penis.

Toft *n.*
A sign that appears to point in more than one direction.

Toller Whelme *n.*
The road sign in front of you that you learned for your driving test, but whose meaning you've long since forgotten.

Tootgarook *n.*
One who retweets praise about themself.

Torremolinos *pl.n.*
Obstacles in a chase scene that hinder the hero: mothers with prams, crowded fruit markets, an entire Mardi Gras parade mysteriously absent from the rest of the scene.

Tralee *n.*
The expression on the face of your cat as it enters the kitchen with a bird in its mouth.

Trambly *adj.*
Chronically anxious due to next door having a superior trampoline.

Trantlebeg *n.*
One who doggedly sticks to the speed they
intend to drive at, no matter how long the line
of cars behind them.

Traquair *v.*
To march purposefully off in entirely the
wrong direction.

Treborth *adj.*
Pregnant with an eco-warrior's child.

Treffort *n.*
A tremendous effort to make something
shorter.

Treflach *n.*
The gold embossing on airport novels.

Tresco *v.*
To dance with the upper body while seated.

Tritteling-Redlach *n.*
The noise made in the throat of a lawyer to
indicate a) the difficulty and b) the expense of
what you require.

Troon *adj.*
Not quite bored enough to switch off the television.

Tubbrid *adj.*
(Of Method actors) In the manner of a potato or Jerusalem artichoke.

Tuckton *n.*
A pair of socks that has been folded into a ball.

Turcifal *n.*
The fat lady who comes on for the opera finale and sings 'The End'.

Turnaspidogy *n.*
The black art of making a TV commercial appear more caring, authentic and honest by adding a regional accent.

Turtmann *n.*
Annoying passenger on

a train who doesn't realise how loudly he's slurping his coffee because he has earphones on.

Tutbury *n.*
An ancient git who glares with barely contained rage at a perfectly well-behaved child in a cinema or on a bus.

Tweed Heads *pl.n.*
People who think about fishing all day.

Tweefontein *n.*
An idea that can only be expressed in 140 characters by abbreviating it in some inelegant way.

Twinhoe *n.*
Person who likes to hang out with twins.

Twitchen *n.*
Someone who can't wait to leave and get back on Twitter.

Ty Croes *n.*
Celebrity whose fame is destined to stay
local. (Literally, 'the Welsh Tom Cruise'.)

Tyringe *n.*
The pin on a security badge found in your
pocket that stabs your finger as a punishment
for not returning it to Reception.

Tyttenhanger *n.*
The matronly lady at the back of an
underwear shop who knows what bra size her
customers are just by looking at them.

U

U

Ubby *n.*
A rotting cricket ball found in the garden under a bush.

Uckerby *n.*
A workmate who will only drink tea out of his own special mug.

Uffcott *n.*
The least popular exit from a roundabout.

Uffington *n.*
Outrageous opinion in a column intended purely to provoke.

Ulbster *n.*
A spot that's ripe to be squeezed.

Ulceby Skitter *n.*
The improbable plot twist in a thriller that leaves you feeling cheated.

Ullatti *pl.n.*
The tiny wooden spades that come with individual tubs of ice cream.

Ullinish *adj.*
Still struggling to finish *Ulysses*.

Ummeracly *adv.*
In the manner of one who remains uncertain how to spell a word that's just been spelled out to them.

Underriver Ho *n.*
Prostitute whose drowned body kick-starts the murder mystery.

Unsworth *n.*
Someone who can't wait to hear your ideas so they can pooh-pooh them.

Upper Froyle *n.*
Raised eyebrow that says 'What the hell do you think you're doing exactly?'

Upper Godney *n.*
The more persistent of two Jehovah's Witnesses at your door.

Upper Swainswick *n.*
The level of management that doesn't do any
work because they spend all day in meetings.

Upton Snodsbury *n.*
An owner who looks like their pet.

Uralla *n.*
A towel used as a bathmat.

Uruguay *interj.*
Angry protest by small boy made to get off the
Xbox before he's finished his level.

Ustibar *n.*
A snack that claims to be healthy, made of
honey, twigs and gravel.

Utrillas *pl.n.*
Luxuriant nostril hairs.

V

Vange *adj.*
The female equivalent of 'phallic'.

Velator *n.*
A ten-year-old boy who can't wait to grow up
to be a banker.

Velving *ptcpl.v.*
Amusing oneself during a massage by trying
to guess which part of their body the person
giving the massage is using.

Venables *pl.n.*
The fingerprints in a sandwich caused by pressing down on it while cutting it in half.

Ventnor *n.*
One who contacts you with the sole purpose of clearing the air and getting things out in the open.

Ventry *n.*
The hole in a belt slightly enlarged by regular use.

Vereeniging *ptcpl.v.*
Making a noise like screeching tyres as you drive round a corner.

Vibble *v.*
To dither around inside a shop after closing time, wondering how long you have left.

Viker *n.*
(ARCHAIC) A motorcycling vicar.

Villagrains *pl.n.*
The crumbs that stop a DVD machine from
working, caused by small children carefully
inserting toast into the slot.

Virming *ptcpl.v.*
In a car park, entering your vehicle sideways
with your stomach held in, because some
bastard has parked too close to you.

Vobster *n.*
The rubbery glue left on glass jars after the
labels have been pulled off.

Void-Vacon *n.*
The important signature on a new driving
licence or credit card that you realise,
halfway through writing, is not going to turn
out right.

Volimes *pl.n.*
People who turn the television up when
eating.

Volmunster *n.*
Norse giant slain by Turcifal (q.v.), Goddess of Plenty, to prevent him revealing to the birds of the air that scarecrows aren't actually people.

Voorst *v.*
To make V-signs at people on television.

VOORST 3,2

Vron Gate *n.*
Opening scene of a sci-fi film, establishing that the world is not as we know it.

Vuku *n.*
The Balinese art of making rooms appear bigger and more numerous, as practised by all the great masters of estate agency.

Walberswick *n.*
The piece of string attached to a tampon.

Walkerburn *n.*
Speedwalker's equivalent of jogger's nipple.

Wallness *n.*
The feeling that you might have been a spider
in a previous life.

Waltham Cross *n.*
A brief unsatisfactory conversation between
two people on adjacent escalators, one going
down and the other going up.

Wapping *ptcpl.v.*
Walking purposefully around the workplace
holding an important-looking piece of paper,
to disguise the fact you have absolutely
nothing to do.

Warlus *n.*
A word you're always uncertain how to spell,
no matter how many times you have to write it.

Weesp *n.*
One who phones in to a radio DJ and then is
too shy to say anything.

Welwick *n.*
The sound of a tent zip that induces nostalgia
for camping.

Wembury *n.*
Momentary curiosity as to what a warning
light on your dashboard is meant to convey.

Wendling *ptcpl.v.*
Ostentatiously sniffing and swirling wine in a
glass.

Wendover *n.*
The point on a family walk when the youngest
bursts into tears and won't go any further.

Westby-with-Plumptons *n.*
The style of speaking pioneered by Brian
Sewell.

Wharfe *n.*
Loud conversation overheard between
successful businessmen who want you
to know you are overhearing successful
businessmen.

Whimble *v.*
To feebly respond to a wave from an unknown
driver of a passing car.

Whitehaven *n.*
An architect's immaculate living space, which
you're frightened to enter in case your breath
leaves a mark.

Wickham Market *n.*
A mental shopping list drafted during sexual
intercourse.

Wickmere *n.*
The wan smile of one given a scented candle
by a visiting aunt.

Wilberfoss *n.*
Mental pressure exerted in an attempt to
make traffic lights go green.

Winfarthing *n.*
The shifty-looking bloke at the fair who glues
down the coconuts.

Winnersh Triangle *n.*
An unfashionable pubic hairstyle.

Winnington *n.*
The sound of cheers carried on the breeze
from a distant sports field.

Witton Gilbert *n.*
An author whose only published book is *An
Author's Guide to Publishing*.

Wiveliscombe *n.*
One who enters a revolving door so absorbed
in texting they end up back out on the street.

Woll *v.*
To tap the walls and make doubtful
murmuring noises as an estate agent shows
you round a property.

Wonersh *n.*
One who insists they don't watch television,
only box sets.

Wookey Hole *n.*
The gap in a slightly too small piece of
wrapping paper, through which part of the gift
can be seen.

Woolloomooloo *n.*
The small, pinkish ball of lint found in the
tumble dryer after washing one's underthings.

Woomera *n.*
A sudden and inexplicable storming out of a
room by a teenager.

Worb *n.*
A familiar word, such as 'weird', that just
doesn't look right the more you stare at it; in
fact it looks weird.

Wotton-under-Edge *n.*
The Marmite below the shoulder of the jar
that can't be reached by a knife and has to be
scooped out with a finger.

Woumen *pl.n.*
Mythical race of women who don't enjoy
leafing through magazines.

Wroxeter *n.*
A text sent to the wrong person.

Wychbold *n.*
The outline of your watch etched into your
wrist.

Wychling *ptcpl.v.*
Adopting the voice of an old crone for the
purposes of panto, children's bedtime story,
imitating partner's mother, etc.

Wyre Piddle *n.*
A small child with its shoes on the wrong
feet.

X

Xining *ptcpl.v.*
Including something beginning with X in an
A–Z list, even if it isn't very interesting.

Y

Yafford *n.*
A dog that walks its owner.

Yàmbol *adj.*
A phone in yàmbol mode repeatedly offers
a symbol instead of the letter or number you
need at a crucial mom±§§*

Yanting *ptcpl.v.*
Exultantly punching the air on waking up in
the morning, gloriously and magnificently
conscious that, once again, you are Bono.

Yarborough *n.*
Repetitive yawn injury caused by over-
exposure to pensions advisers.

Yardley Gobion *n.*
The sticky trail of detritus running between
back door and dustbin.

Yarpole *n.*
The distance from their nose that a person too
vain to wear reading glasses holds a menu or
newspaper.

Yasnomorsky *n.*
One who gives sensible answers all the way
through the census form and then spoils it at
the end by putting his religion down as 'Jedi'.

Yaxham *n.*
A bib covered in milky vomit.

Yealand Conyers *pl.n.*
People haltingly trying to communicate
with each other in a foreign language before
realising they're all English.

Yeo *v.*
To swerve without warning from one lane to
another in a hired van.

Yepes *interj.*
The last statement of a squashed hedgehog.

Youlgreave *n.*
A word disconcertingly misread for another,

as in 'The Prime Minister was breastfeeding at Chequers' instead of 'breakfasting'.

Yoxford *n.*
The special beam in a country cottage you always hit your head on.

Ypsilanti *n.*
Group of recently discharged mental patients at a bus stop.

Yspytty Cynfyn *n.*
A conversation between two people brushing their teeth.

Z

Zaltbommel n.
Expensive wooden toy, solid in design, designed to be attractive to parents but which the children are going to hate.

Zanzibar n.
To temporarily forget alphabetical order and find yourself looking something up in Z.

Zeanor n.
A decision requiring intensive, immediate and complex calculations; the opposite of a no-brainer.

Zevikon n.
The sound and smell of freshly-sawn wood.

Zigter n.
One who sidles up to your table with wares for sale.

Z

Zaltbommel *n.*
Expensive wooden toy sold in Geneva airport
designed to be attractive to parents but which
the children are going to hate.

Zanzibar *v.*
To temporarily forget alphabetical order when
looking something up in an index.

Zennor *n.*
A decision requiring immense thought and
complex calculations; the opposite of a 'no
brainer'.

Zezikon *n.*
The sound and smell of freshly sawn timber.

Zigler *n.*
One who sidles up to your table with roses for
sale.

Zinasco *n.*
Road accident caused by watching a row of zeros coming up on the milometer.

Zolling *ptcpl.v.*
Of shop assistants, averting the eyes in a theatrical manner as the customer enters their PIN.

Zouch *n.*
A panicky nocturnal thought that makes you suddenly sit up in bed.

Zububa *n.*
The enormous amount of unnecessary stuff men bring back from the supermarket.

Zugdidi *n.*
The last dirty cup that materialises just after you start the dishwasher.

Zumpango *n.*
No idea. Could be a vegetable?

ACKNOWLEDGEMENTS

The authors extend their grateful thanks to the many people whose brilliant definitions helped to make *Afterliff* such fun to compile. From Australia, Finland, Germany, India, Ireland, the Netherlands, New Zealand, South Africa, Spain, Sweden, Turkey and the USA (as well as the UK) they are the inspiration for one-fifth of the book.

AUTHOR CREDITS

With one liff each: Tanya Almor; Robin Armstrong; Craig E. E. Barber; Simon Beasor; Simon Bennett; Robin Bonass; Dave Boulting; P. J. Bristow; Holly Brockwell; Lee Brown; Bob Bury; Granny Buttons; Michael John Byrne; Oz Cable; Jo Capon; Neil Carruthers; James Cary; Mark Case; Gordon Chapman-Fox; Ian Cocks; The Reverend Richard Coles; Robyn Colquhoun; Catherine 'Beehive' Crick; Alan Crow; Mark Cummings, BBC Radio Gloucestershire; A. J. Dehany; Robin Denham; Meha

Desai; Roger Downing; David Dowson; Ron Edmonds; Ann Edwards; Graham Edwards; Rita Elliott; Dominic Ely; Dr Liam Farrell; Lisa Featherstone; Mick Freed; Kevin J. Frost; Janet Georgiou; Jamie Gladden; Helen Goddard; Lee Gosling; Christopher Gray; David Haddock; Hannah Hart; @neiljhenry; Simon Holland-Roberts; Chris Hook; Cathy Hurren; Matthew Imrie; Robert Jack; @nickkemptown; Andrew Icon Kerr; Nick Land; Chris Limb; Simon Linnell; Paul R. Livesey; Booty Lloyd; Harry Lloyd; Mark Loftus; Andrew Lowes; Felicity Luxmoore; Susie Lydon; Hazel Lyth; Andrew MacCormack; Stephen Marsland; Cian Masterton; Chris McCrohan; Jo McGowan; Stephen McIlvenna; Joe McLachlan; Elf McNeil; Stewart McSporran; David Metzger; Gordon Miller; Kate Molins; Ben Moore; Sam Moorwood; Jim Mortleman; Clive Murray; Keith W. Myerscough; Gawain Nash; Kerry Chriss Nicholls; Kirsty O' Callaghan; Andy O'Neil; Dave Parkinson; Gary J. Payne; Jeremy 'JPoems' Peacock; Oliver Percivall; Melanie Powell; Catherine Prescott; Falko Rademacher; John Ranson; Rick Rayson; Pete Rieden; Dr Mike Robinson; Tuula Ruskeeniemi; Richard Sandling; Sarah Shotts; Erin Slack; Steve

Smith; Daran Stebbing; Jacqueline Steel; Wesley Stinson; David Stokes; Chris Stone; Neil James Tarrant; Janette Keene Taylor; Sue Teddern; Sarah Thomasin; Ian Tilly; Hanneke du Toit; Ian Tollett; Shadric Toop; Karen Siân Wall; Terry Washburn; Cleve West; Thom White; Simon Williams (Bard of Exeter 2013); Keith A. Wilson (@keith_wilson); Maggie Woodward. **With two liffs each**: Marion Beet; Steven Brooker; Alan Byrne; Philip Calvert; Jon Culshaw; Anthony Denny; Richard 'Reg' Gray; Jules Heynes; Peter Hildebrand; Mikey Jackson; Andra Jenkin; Dylan Kesler; Hannah O'Byrne; Seylan Öztürk; Lev Parikian; Emma Summers; Kerry Tucker; Richard Vidal; Lindsay Warner. **With three liffs each**: Garrick Alder; Alexander Burrows; Ian Cattell; Jenny Doughty; Doug Forrest; Maria de Haas ('yorz); Dave Higgins; Aidan Maccormick; David Martyn; Nick (tetsabb) McD; Karissa McLaverty; Celebaelin (Alun Roberts); Craig Warhurst. **With four liffs each**: Dylan Beattie; Jon Brierley; Dave Dexter; Ashley L. V. Smith; Katherine Vick; Andrew Wyld. **With five liffs each**: James Harkin and Guy Rundle. **And with six liffs each**: Sanjeev Bhaskar and Astrid Malachewitz (AlmondFacialBar).

Having worked solidly on this book together for over six months, the authors know just how difficult it is to come up with *one* liff, let alone more than six of them. An admiring and respectful tipton (q.v.) then to the true lifferati below:

Jules Bailey (nine liffs); Helen Fielding, Piers Fletcher and Andrew Sunnucks (ten liffs each); @babydrums (thirteen liffs); Chris Blackwell (fourteen liffs); Stewart Harrison and Phil Lawrence (seventeen liffs each); Stephen Yately (eighteen liffs); and last, but over-emphatically very far from least indeed, Felicity 'Swot' Lewis and Joseph Moorwood, each with an astounding twenty-nine liffs.

We would particularly like to thank Joe Moorwood for his kind permission to use excerpts from his charming but as yet unpublished work *The Book of Yorkshire Liffs*. We will be delighted to pass on his details to any interested parties.

DISCLAIMER
Strenuous efforts have been made to contact all the authors of the definitions in this book. If we have failed to reach you, please contact us as soon as possible at www.afterliff.com. Pleasant surprises await.

ILLUSTRATIONS

Thanks to all those budding Cartier-Bressons who kindly responded to our appeal for signposts from round the world that appear within.

Their work has been selected and collated by Chris Gray (QI's IT and Photography Elf) who not only snapped twelve of the signposts himself, but is also, as it happens, the author of the very first entry in *Afterliff*.

PHOTO CREDITS

With one picture each: James Brewer; Phil Brown; Sara Cannon; Chris Clipson; Mick Freed; Susan Green; Pete Houston; Duncan Jennings; Peter Lamb; David Lines; Paul Livesey; Andy Martin; Heather and Ronan McNamee; Alasdair Miller; Alan Murray; Mary Odurny; Lucy Parry; Meghan Robertson; Peter Rogers; Paul Slootman; Matt Sutton; Simon Wilcock; Cameron Young. **With two pictures each**: James Harkin; Simon Harriyott; Emma Jeddere-Fisher; Linda Jenkins; Rosemary Lynch; Christian Nicholas; Anna-Maria Oléhn; Stuart Pearcey. **With three pictures each**: Heather Briggs; Belinda Taylor. **And with four pictures each**: Dave Ackrill and Phil Lawrence.

Space prevented more photos being included, but we hope to feature them all on www.afterliff.com in due course.

SPECIAL THANKS
These acknowledgements would be hopelessly inadequate without a fulsome mention of Beth O'Dea, the wonderfully gifted producer of BBC Radio 4's *The Meaning Of Liff At 30*; Nigel Bayley, the calmly indefatigable curator of Twitter's @ThatsLiff; and our friends Robbie Stamp and Steve Dunkley of Douglas Adams' amazing website h2g2.com. Without their unstinting generosity and inventiveness, this would have been an unrecognisably different and vastly less liffish book.

WITHOUT WHOM
Finally, thanks of a particularly gushing and lip-trembly variety are due to our multi-capable editorial assistant and amanuensis, Andrew Hunter Murray. Words, even liff words, can hardly describe his amazing work-rate, buzzard-eyed perception, patience, charm and grace under fire. It is unimaginable to consider how impossible it would have been to assemble *Afterliff* without him. Not only that, he is

talented too: a full thirty-seven of the definitions in this book are his own, unaided work. If he weren't so nice, he'd be seriously annoying.

A NOTE ON DUPLICATIONS

Keen-eyed liff buffs may notice that thirteen place names from *The Deeper Meaning of Liff* (republished in the autumn of 2013 by Macmillan as an omnibus hardback edition of *The Meaning of Liff*) also appear in *Afterliff*: Clathy, Clun, Eakring, Godalming, Hastings, Lostwithiel, Nantwich, Peening Quarter, Polyphant, Shimpling, Sittingbourne, Swaffham Bulbeck and Ventnor. This is wholly intentional: in Liffish, as in English, words can (and do) have multiple meanings.

APPEAL FOR ENTRIES/WEBSITE ETC

We've so enjoyed the process of collaborating with anonymous (and immensely creative) members of the public on this book that we wonder if a fourth incarnation of *Liff* might be possible one day.

You can start this process by having a look at www.afterliff.com. We're looking for new ideas for definitions and (especially) hope to gather a signpost photograph for every liff in both of the books.

INDEX OF MEANINGS

A

A4: *Geddington*
ABRIDGEMENTS
 elegant: *Treffort*
 inelegant: *Tweefontein*
ACCENTS
 amateur-dramatic:
 Schwentinental
 Anglo-French: *Beausemblant*
 upper-class: *Brompton Ralph*
ACCIDENTS
 email: *Sentosa*
 frightening: *Heckmondwike*
 genital: *Climping*
ACRONYMS: *Morfa*
ACTORS
 emoting deeply: *Hoff*
 impersonating a potato:
 Tubbrid
ADDRESS BOOKS: *Aachen, Aast*
ADULTERY: *Humbug Scrub*
ADVERTISEMENTS
 brief: *Adbolton*
 caring: *Turnaspidogy*
 deceptive: *Quernmore*
 shouty: *Heglibister*
 sofa: *Muchlarrick*
AGREEMENTS
 grudging: *Plaistow*
 vague: *Memel*
AIR, clearing the: *Ventnor*
ALARM CLOCKS: *Belmont*
ALCOHOL: *Aberglasney*
ALPHA MALES: *Pont-y-Pant*

AMERICANS
 bizarre pronunciation by:
 Hreppholar
 bright future of: *Aston Clinton*
ANGER
 enjoyable: *High Ireby*
 childish: *Uruguay*
ANIMALS
 unidentifiable remains of: *Stroat*
 upgraded housing of: *Cruft*
ANSWERS
 crisp, sensible: *Thornton Steward*
 robotic, useless: *Belltrees*
APOSTROPHES: *Longhedge*
APPLES: *Newton Mearns*
APRONS, amusing: *Briffons*
ARCHAEOLOGY, dull: *Carrogs*
ARCHER, JEFFREY: *Briscous*
ARCHITECTS: *Whitehaven*
ARGOS: *Poringland*
ARGUMENTS
 insincere: *Bulwell*
 making up after: *Toames*
ARMCHAIRS
 dents in: *Sittingbourne*
 noises made when sinking into:
 Guilden Sutton
 old ladies asleep in: *Gradgery*
ART, GENITAL: *Murist*
ARTICHOKES, Method: *Tubbrid*
ASSURANCES, smooth: *Solent Breezes*
ATHEISM: *Hugus*
AUSTEN, JANE: *Lydiard Millicent*
AUTHORS, rubbish: *Witton Gilbert*

B

BABIES
  aromatic: *Bebeah*
  hideous: *Gawcott*
  of indeterminate gender:
  Boufflers
  rattle-wielding: *Cottered*
  ticklish: *Killybegs*
BACON, ooze from: *Knill*
BADGES, vengeful: *Tyringe*
BAGS for life: *Nudgee*
BALLOONS: *Blaby*
BALLS
  cock and: *Murist*
  cricket: *Ubby*
  tennis: *Nibun*
BANANAS, Canadian: *Banada*
BANDS
  disbanded: *Terryglass*
  tribute: *Aberdovey*
  wrist: *Jamberoo*
BANISTERS: *Hampstead*
BANKERS
  future: *Velator*
  past: *Templeshambo*
  present: *Chuffily-Roche*
BASEBALL CAPS: *Hatfield*
BATHS
  squeaky clean after: *Clathy*
  weight gain during: *Dropmore*
BATTERIES: *Godalming*
BEARDS
  kissing with: *Mungo Brush*
  probably glued on: *Nymet Tracey*
BED, extra time in: *Brixworth*
BEGGARS: *Chettle*
BIBS: *Yaxham*
BIGOTS: *Cumledge*
BILLIONAIRES: *Clyst Honiton*
BIROS
  use of in espionage: *Quilquox*
  things which aren't: *Scrivelsby*
  utterly despicable: *Scrooby*

BISCUITS
  dunked: *Silsden*
  Lincoln: *Froncles*
BISHOPS: *Bishop's Nympton*
BLINDS: *Frome*
BLISTERS: *Gloucester*
BLOWING UP
  balloons: *Blaby*
  bottoms: *Smoke Hole*
BOARD GAMES, complicated:
  Hanbury
BOBBLES, nautical: *Fomperron*
BODIES, unexpected parts of:
  Beattock
BOG, *see* LAVATORY
BOGGLE: *Skeffling*
BOLLYWOOD: *Agharoo*
BONFIRES: *Dolving*
BONNETS: *Blindcrake*
BONO: *Yanting*
BOOKS
  badly reviewed on Amazon:
  Manaus
  bought for your partner: *Meon*
  bought but not read: *King's
  Newton*
  with flashy embossing: *Treflach*
BOOKSHOPS, hilarious pranks in
  second-hand: *Sargasso*
BORES
  nostalgic: *Ashby Puerorum*
  repetitive: *Hinton Waldrist*
  sinister: *Stratford Tony*
BOTTOMS
  bare naked ladies': *Huish*
  mooning gnomes': *Briffons*
  prodding: *Soppog*
BOXES
  cardboard: *Kingledoors*
  chocolate: *Bermuda*
  match: *Scatsta*
  thinking outside of: *Carse of
  Lecropt*
BOYS
  playing cops and robbers:

Pyongyang
pretending to be aeroplanes:
Little Stukeley
pulling faces: *Gurnard*
BRAS
instantly sized-up: *Tyttenhanger*
tangled: *Aughnaloopy*
worn over sweaters: *Melcombe
Horsey*
BRIEFCASES: *Martin Hussingtree*
BUBBLES
bath: *Flothers*
speech: *Quetico*
BUDGET, the: *Stathe*
BUILDERS, tidy: *Brixham*
BUILDINGS, that look like
something else: *Simister*
BUSES
bells on: *Bussnang*
drunks on: *Inchmahome*
BUTCHERS: *Cherry Burton*
BUTTONS
metaphorical: *Nether Button*
pointless: *Putton*
poppable: *Prestatyn*

C

CABIN CREW: *Clayton*
CAFES
cosy sofas in: *Furzey Lodge*
crud left on tables of: *Scurdie
Ness*
unattended counters in:
Strawberry Bank
wet cushions in: *Basket Swamp*
wet tables in: *Plean*
CAFETIERES
time-consuming: *Barnawartha*
treacherous: *Flyford Flavell*
CAMERA FILM, undeveloped: *Rhyl*
CAMPING, unforgettable: *Welwick*
CANAPES, unidentifiable: *Beltana*
CANDLES, unwanted: *Wickmere*

CAR ALARMS, unmourned:
Garmelow
CAR KEYS: *Lewisham*
CARDS
birthday: *Scatness*
Christmas: *Dinkelhausen*
credit, see **CREDIT**
post: *Smailholm*
CARNIVORES: *Duckend Green*
CARS
old: *East Anglia*
very old: *Simoda*
CATCHPHRASES: *Molepolole*
CATS
facial expressions of: *Tralee*
gloop left on the floor by: *Kittitoe*
CELEBRITIES
closely-encountered: *Meuthop*
easily-identified: *Ogdens*
locally-restricted: *Ty Croes*
CELLOPHANE: *Plenisette*
CEMETERIES: *Hartley Mauditt*
CENSUSES: *Yasnomorsky*
CHAIRS
garden, designer: *Ingleby
Greenhow*
garden, winter: *Inverness*
go-faster: *Barjarg*
CHANTS, sacred: *Alawoona*
CHARITIES
tax-efficient: *Goodrich*
vaguely-named: *Scopus*
CHASTITY: *Barwick-in-Elmet*
CHEAP, disturbingly: *Bricy*
CHECKOUTS, garrulous: *Gorbals*
CHEERS: *Winnington*
CHEESE
cottage: *Lechlade*
prongs in: *Spen*
smidgeons of: *Peatling Parva*
twirly: *Haselbury Plucknett*
CHEESEGRATERS, injuries caused
by: *Macerata*
CHESS
end-games: *King's Pyon*

[193]

horse-play: *Galapian*
mind-games: *Castleruddery*

CHICKENS
belligerent: *Cappananty*
frozen: *Pluckley*

CHILDREN
beastly: *Rathcrogue*
former: *Little Kelk*
inept: *Hurlet*
opinionated: *Loudwater*
sporty: *Boyanup*
treacherous: *Niederbipp*

CHILLIS: *Brombos*

CHINS
double: *Crowle*
prehensile: *Chinley*

CHIPS: *Fritton*

CHIRPINESS, irritating: *Henty*

CHOCOLATES, shunned: *Bermuda*

CHRISTMAS
cards: *Dinkelhausen*
lights: *Mevagissey*
presents: *Sepon*

CIGARETTE, time elapsed since
your last: *Beagle Gulf*

CINEMA, shushers in the: *Lulworth
Cove*

CLAPPING, in the wrong sort of
silence: *Inverlune*

CLOTHING
beige: *Dunwear*
experimental: *Nelling*
sloppy: *Crunwear*
tags on: *Pluckanes*

CLOVERS: *Clovulin*

CLOWNS, Italian: *Gribbio*

CLUBS
awful people in: *Kenmare*
ghastly gloom after: *Clun*

COATHANGERS, sentient: *Naddle*

COCKNEYS: *Kennythorpe*

COCONUTS, the bloke who glues
down the: *Winfarthing*

CODENAMES, genital: *Clunbury*

COFFEE, scalding: *Flyford Flavell*

COFFINS: *St Serf's Inch*

COINS
low value: *Devizes*
no value: *Cashel*

COLLEAGUES, fatuous: *The Knab*

COLONIC IRRIGATION:
Poughkeepsie

COMMUTERS: *Spaxton*

COMPLAINTS
awkward silences after:
Harpenden
hypocritical: *Tittybong*
ill-informed: *Balranald*
pre-emptive: *Cumberworth*

COMPUTING: *Bracknell*

CONDOMS: *Sand Hutton*

CONGREGATIONS
mumbling: *Hemel Hempstead*
scanty: *Alvechurch*

CONNERY, SIR SEAN: *Grishipoll*

CONSTELLATIONS: *Scarasta*

CONTACT LENSES, things which
aren't: *Flashader*

CONVERSATIONS
ostentatious: *Wharfe*
premarital: *Much Wenlock*
self-obsessed: *Meigle*
spittle-flecked: *Yspytty Cynfyn*
standing too close for: *Inworth*
wise nods during: *Isbister*

COTTAGE
beams: *Yoxford*
cheese: *Lechlade*

COTTON BUDS, orange: *Amcotts*

COUPLES
brother and sister: *Symbister*
near and far: *Thirroul*
tall and short: *Pipe and Lyde*

COURAGE, pathetic excuse for:
Timbold

COWELL, SIMON: *Portsoy*

CREDIT CARDS
alternative use for: *Carlton
Scroop*
anxiety during normal use:

Herning
avoiding looking at: *Zolling*
crap signatures on: *Void-Vacon*
CRICKET
balls: *Ubby*
fans: *Attymon*
motorcycles: *Midsomer Norton*
CRISP, QUENTIN: *Campo Grande*
CRITICISM
enjoyable, vicious, behind back:
Amby
unenjoyable, self-, after party:
Boloquoy
CROISSANTS, not: *Broons*
CROSSINGS
off: *Lispopple*
Pelican: *Acaster Malbis*
CROSSWORDS
cheating at: *Fimber*
infuriated by: *Annagry*
CRUMBS
beneath toasters: *Largs*
deep inside DVD machines:
Villagrains
C***: *Clent*
CURTAINS
exuberant swishing of: *Suishnish*
premature opening of:
Brightlingsea
CUSTOMS: *Crimby*

D

DACHSHUNDS: *Datchet*
DANCING
not even slightly: *Cocking
Causeway*
sedentary: *Tresco*
to adjust pants: *Diggle*
to put trousers on: *Mockerkin*
DASHBOARDS: *Blindcrake*
DECISIONS, incredibly difficult
and important: *Zennor*
DÉJÀ VU: *Balerno*

DENTISTS
sparkling dialogue with: *Ouyen*
parting remarks to: *Ljubljana*
DENTS
in armchairs: *Sittingbourne*
in fingers: *Penzance*
in jackets: *Pocklington*
in noses: *Aismunderby*
DESSERT: *Bowlish*
DIETS, weight gain during:
Maesycrugiau
DIM SUM: *Hong*
DINGS: *Attunga*
DIRECTION, wrong: *Traquair*
DISEASES
amateur, venereal: *Kirk Smeaton*
professional, venereal:
Thrashbush
DISENGAGEMENT
from a cello: *Debach*
from a wedgie: *Lower Sheering*
DISHWASHERS: *Zugdidi*
DISLIKE, irrational: *Goodworth
Clatford*
DITHERING: *Vibble*
DIVERS, ex-: *Dover*
DIVORCE: *Amesbury*
DODGEMS: *Bempton*
DOGS
pernickety owners of:
Stubbington
prancing owners of: *Thurning*
rogering: *Kuala Lumpur*
sleeping: *Tobermory*
straining: *Yafford*
twitching: *Barooga*
DOORS
revolving: *Wiveliscombe*
unattached: *Skelton*
DOUBLE ACTS: *Strubby with
Woodthorpe*
DOUGHNUTS: *Bunratty*
DREAMS
doggy: *Tobermory*
human: *Belmont, Burlats*

DRINKS
  disappointingly small: *Tidworth*
  more than enough: *Lostock Junction*
  with bits of sandwich in: *Cobnash*

DRIVING
  doggedly: *Trantlebeg*
  erratically: *Yeo*

DRONING, historical: *Beeston*

DRUGS, anal: *Nether Stowey*

DRUMS, bass: *Jimboomba*

DRUNKS: *Inchmahome*

DUCKS: *Canaples*

DVDs
  not working: *Villagrains*
  working: *Stonganess*

E

EARS, dribbling: *Ewloe*

EGGS, tapping: *Oving*

ELDERLY
  adverts aimed at the: *Grayshott*
  beige clothes worn by the: *Dunwear*
  denial of napping by the: *Gradgery*
  explanation of computers to the: *Bracknell*

ELTON JOHN, SIR, the glamorous life of: *Flothers*

EMAILS
  disastrous: *Sentosa*
  saucy: *Friskney*

ENEMIES
  surly nods to: *Boasley Cross*
  warm greetings from: *Old Edlington*

ENTHUSIASM
  lack of, in cockerels: *Henlow*
  lack of, in general: *Ab Lench*

ENTOURAGES, precocious: *Licola*

ENVIRONMENT, lukewarm concern for: *Seave Green*

ESCALATORS
  conversations on: *Waltham Cross*
  inhabitants of: *Freuchies*

ESTATE AGENTS
  duplicity of: *Fentral*
  further duplicity of: *Vuku*
  how to irritate: *Woll*

EXES
  pangs over: *Hüffenhardt*
  perfect: *Studley Roger*
  porky partners of: *Hüffelsheim*

EXPLETIVES
  barely worthy of the name: *Hassocks*
  inserted: *Scunthorpe*
  reluctant: *Clent*

EYE CONTACT, disturbing: *Croome*

EYEBROWS
  individual hairs of: *Skares*
  raised: *Upper Froyle*

EYES
  closed: *Drewton*
  lazy: *Anglesey*
  locked: *Croome*
  smokey: *Dolving*
  theatrically averted: *Zolling*

F

FACES
  claustrophobic: *Inworth*
  contorted: *Gelligroes*
  pulling: *Gurnard*
  singer-songwriters': *Harburn*

FAECES
  in potty: *Enderby*
  in transit: *Humptulips*

FAIRGROUNDS: *Winfarthing*

FAIRTRADE: *Swaythling*

FAMILY
  gatherings: *Peening Quarter*
  genealogy: *Manningtree*

FANCY DRESS, hopeless: *Flappit Spring*

GERMANS
  naked: *Letheringsett*
  plentiful: *Hungladder*
GESTURES
  Mongolian: *Rhughasinish*
  telephonic: *Barlin*
GIANTS
  Newtonian: *Newtonmore*
  Norse: *Volmunster*
  nostrils of: *Metricup*
GIFT SHOPS, empty: *Esquerchin*
GLARES
  from concert-goers: *Inverlune*
  from old gits on buses: *Tutbury*
  from Scotsmen in pubs:
  McGregor's Corner
  from tea-drinkers: *Teevurcher*
  from unused landlines: *Sulham*
  towards inanimate objects: *Neen
  Savage*
GLASSES
  dents in nose from: *Aismunderby*
  resemblance to superhero from:
  Drimmo
  thick-rimmed: *Daggons*
  too vain to wear: *Yarpole*
GLOVE COMPARTMENTS: *Annecy*
GLOVES
  children's: *Hampole*
  oven: *Caterham*
  percussionists': *Mittagong*
  scented: *Humptulips*
GNOMES, garden: *Briffons*
GOALS: *Prowse*
GOATS, things that aren't: *Chambilly*
GOD: *Abbots Ripton*
GOLFERS, insane: *Ballywatticock*
GOODBYES, botched: *Gomersal*
GOSSIP: *Belmunging*
GRAFFITI: *Murist*
GRAPES: *Kangarilla*
GREETINGS
  equine: *Haigh*
  half-rising: *Chertsey*
  intermittent: *Hallon*

GUESTS, who pretend they've been
  shot: *Obergurgl*
GURUS, glasses of management:
  Daggons
GUY OF GISBORNE: *Guith*
GYMS: *Rickmansworth*

H

HAIR
  fiddling with: *Crindle*
  lunatic tufts of: *Kiel Crofts*
HANDBAGS: *Nelsherry*
HANDSHAKES
  creepy: *Creevins*
  watery: *Kirby-le-Soken*
HARRY POTTER: *Quidnish*
HATS
  imaginary doffing of: *Tipton*
  papal: *Caterham*
  off but doesn't feel like it:
  Hatfield
  with ears on: *Cradley*
  worn by buffoons riding donkeys:
  Dutson
HEADPHONES: *Jackadgery*
HEDGEHOGS: *Yepes*
HEIGHT
  differences in: *Pipe and Lyde*
HELP, not bloody likely: *Faccombe*
HERBS, inability to say the word:
  Hreppholar
HIDE-AND-SEEK: *Malahide*
HOLES
  in aeroplane windows: *Frasseto*
  in arses: *Smoke Hole*
  in bedroom walls: *Oodnadatta*
  in belts: *Ventry*
  in golf courses: *Micheldever*
  in presents: *Wookey Hole*
HOLIDAYS
  failure of tan on: *Caramany*
  flow of time on: *Ebberston*
HOMOSEXUALITY: *Quatsino*

HONEY, foreign objects in: *Beelsby*
HORSES
  light conversation between:
  Haigh
  squiggles which don't resemble:
  Horse of Copinsay
HOTELS
  ambiguous liquids provided by:
  Aruba
  fluffiness of towels in: *Abernethy*
  forgettable art in: *Painswick*
  minuscule bathrooms in:
  Monzambano
HUGS: *Leoh*
HYPOCHONDRIA: *Kilkeary*

I

ICE CREAM: *Ullatti*
IGNORANCE, general: *Lostwithiel*
IMPLEMENTS
  agricultural: *Cowhythe*
  cosmetic: *Clayton*
  kitchen: *Danby Wiske*
  tavern: *Broadwoodwidger*
IMPROVEMENTS, catastrophic:
  Birtle
IN OUR TIME: *Keith Inch*
INCOMPETENCE: *Swanbister*
INDEX, keeping up with The Dow
  Jones: *Alawoona*
INNOCENCE, protestations of:
  Snaresbrook
INSECTS: *Antist*
INSTRUCTION MANUALS: *Erquery*
INTERNET
  fear and loathing on the: *Fowey*
  feeble marketing on the:
  Egremont
  repellent postings on the:
  Nutgrove
  self-diagnosis on the: *Illies*
  spelling misteaks on the: *Low
  Snaygill*

whirligig graphic thingies on the:
  Sorrento
INVEIGLING: *Dunoon*
IRON
  brown marks left by an:
  Fryerning
  corrugated: *Ribble*
ITALIANS, *see* WAITERS: *Gribbio*

J

JACKETS
  asinine: *Foscot*
  bovine: *Biggleswade*
  canine: *Datchet*
JARS
  Duchy: *Chadbury*
  sticky: *Vobster*
JEDIS, pretend: *Yasnomorsky*
JEHOVAH'S WITNESSES,
  persistent: *Upper Godney*
JIGSAW, pieces: *Clontumpher*
JOBS
  former, financial: *Bankhead*
  obscure, film: *Chanlockfoot*
JOKES
  from the boss: *Davidson's Mains*
  from the Bard: *Pepper Arden
  Bottoms*
JOURNALISTS: *Askham Bryan*

K

KETTLES: *Macroom*
KETTLING, benign: *Kirtling*
KEYBOARDS
  broken bits of: *Caputh*
  gunk in: *Strood*
KISSES
  bearded: *Mungo Brush*
  bungled: *Dongolocking*
  unshaven: *Burzy*
  unwanted: *Salmon Gums*

very definitely unwanted: *Spittal of Glenmuick*

KITCHEN
  ceilings: *Danby Wiske*
  drawers: *Rissington*
KNIGHTS, lusty: *Barwick-in-Elmet*
KNIVES, hunting: *Cutsyke*
KNOBS
  staircase: *Hampstead*
  stopwatch: *Chetnole*

L

LABELS
  dry-cleaning: *Sezincote*
  maddening: *Queets*
LADYBOYS: *Philippines*
LANDLINES, archaic: *Sulham*
LANGUAGE
  body: *Sychtyn*
  foreign: *Yealand Conyers*
LAP-DANCING: *Letchworth*
LAPTOPS, glow of: *Swona*
LAUGHS, carefree little: *Farthinghoe*
LAVATORY, *see* **LOO**
LEAFLETS
  littering the hall: *Grayshott*
  littering the street: *Adjungbilly*
LEGO: *Kirkwhelpington*
LETTERS
  missing: *Ancaster*
  thank-you: *Alkipi*
LIGHTS
  misleadingly singular: *Carlops*
  momentarily intriguing: *Wembury*
  murderously alluring: *Glims Holm*
  small and nothing to worry about: *Brighton*
LINT: *Woolloomooloo*
LIPSTICK: *Avonmouth*
LIQUIDS
  dubious: *Aruba*

separated: *Binegar*
spilt: *Sweening*
LISTS
  mental: *Wickham Market*
  To Do: *Lispopple*
LOLLIES: *Cricklewood*
LOO, *see* **TOILETS**
LOOKS
  belligerent, from poultry: *Cappananty*
  baleful, from people: *Killiecrankie*
LOTTERY: *Slattocks*
LOVERS: *Symbister*

M

MAIL, junk: *Chevening*
MAKE-UP
  overdone: *Avonmouth*
  overgenerous: *Clayton*
MANAGEMENT, good-for-nothing: *Upper Swainswick*
MANHOLE COVERS, grandiose: *Marganure*
MANUALS, electrical: *Erquery*
MARKS
  and Spencer: *Gussage St Michael*
  left by an iron: *Fryerning*
MARMITE
  inaccessible blobs of: *Wotton-under-Edge*
  secret ingredient of: *Portsoy*
MASSAGE: *Velving*
MASTURBATION, groundwork for: *Fletching*
MATCHBOXES: *Scatsta*
MEAT, of uncertain origin: *Minsk*
MEMBERSHIP: *Drumnadrochit*
MEN
  housework botched by: *Husbands Bosworth*
  housework completed by: *Himbleton*

[200]

MENU
    unlike description on the: *Potto*
    unlike everything else on the:
        Curry Rivel
MESS: *Muckle Skerry*
METAL DETECTORS: *Narridy*
MILOMETERS, hypnotic: *Zinasco*
MINIATURISTS, Flemish: *Compton Pauncefoot*
MISANTHROPY: *Brouchy*
MONEY
    in birthday cards: *Scatness*
    see also **COINS**
MOODS, indeterminate: *Brund*
MOORS, non-Shakespearean:
        Exmoor
MOTHERS
    blethering on: *Meckering*
    concealing hated presents:
        Kadnook
MOTORBIKES
    vicarage: *Viker*
    vintage: *Midsomer Norton*
MOUSTACHE, Hitler's: *Sculms*
MUD: *Cumberland*
MUGS
    false teeth in: *Eccup*
    marks on furniture made by: *Sinton*
    special: *Uckerby*
MUMBLING
    apologetic: *Surrey*
    incoherent: *Omdurman*
    religious: *Hemel Hempstead*
    venomous: *Boasley Cross*
MUMMIES, yummy: *Pennyvennie*
MUSIC, deafening: *Rhydding*

N

NAMES
    fake, in phone address book:
        Aachen
    not spoken as written: *Arkansas*
    obscure, on souvenir mugs:
        Corlattylannan
    ornate American: *Huish Champflower*
    overuse of personal: *Johnby*
NAPPIES: *Hanging Grimston*
NEIGHBOURS
    newsworthiness of: *Stockleigh Pomeroy*
    trampolines of: *Trambly*
NICENESS, insufficient: *Clovelly*
NICKNAMES
    girly: *Poplars*
    irksome, blokey: *The Knab*
NOISES
    admiring: *Geurie*
    aquatic: *Cagnoncles*
    clinking: *Colston Bassett*
    cutlery-basketish: *Killinardrish*
    dreamy: *Burlats*
    jaunty: *Bingley*
    juvenile: *Pyongyang*
    legal: *Tritteling-Redlach*
    magaziney: *Philadelphia*
    tyre: *Vereeniging*
NORSE GIANTS: *Volmunster*
NOSES
    bumping: *Dongolocking*
    denting: *Aismunderby*
    trumpeting: *Honeybugle*
NOSTRIL HAIR
    absent: *Antrim*
    ornamental: *Utrillas*
NOTEBOOKS: *Milverton*
NUDISTS
    English: *Frisby on the Wreake*
    German: *Letheringsett*
    inadvertent: *Nunkeeling*
NUTS, dangerous: *Corippo*

O

OBESITY, sex and: *Glutton Bridge*
OBITUARIES, magnetic:
        Herserange

OBJECTS, irretrievable: *Netheravon*
OBSTACLE COURSES: *Salterhebble*
OFFICES
    walking around importantly in:
    Wapping
    wasting other people's money in:
    Dorking
OLD ETONIANS: *Quinton*
OPERA: *Turcifal*
OPINIONS
    parental: *Loudwater*
    poisonous: *Cumledge*
    pompous: *Newton Poppleford*
    provocative: *Uffington*
    put off till later: *Polegate*
ORANGES, non-orange bits of:
    Stranocum
ORGANISATIONS, crap: *Krumlin*
ORIFICES, unexpected: *Love*
    Clough
OUTPATIENTS: *Ypsilanti*
OVERHEARING: *Hinton Ampner*
OYSTERS: *Oyster Skerries*

P

PACKAGES, weightless: *Albox*
PACKAGING
    impossibly tangled:
    Stranagappoge
    ludicrously pretentious:
    Haselbury Plucknett
PANTIES, tinned: *Briffons*
PANTS
    fitting snugly: *Diggle*
    inside-out: *Pontypool*
PARAGRAPHS, incomprehensible:
    Espelette
PARKING
    close: *Virming*
    free: *Timbo*
PARTIES
    directions to: *Poynings*
    leftovers from: *Rooking*

PASSENGERS
    attractive, reflected in window:
    Eyeworth
    unattractive, slurping coffee:
    Turtmann
PASSING TRAINS: *Didcot Parkway*
PASSPORTS: *Smeeth*
PAST LIVES: *Wallness*
PASTA
    adamantine: *Hosta*
    modish: *Baghetti*
PATRON SAINTS: *St Veep*
PAVEMENTS, blocked:
    Clignancourt
PENCILS, broken: *Scremby*
PENISES
    chocolate: *Briffons*
    minuscule: *Anthorn*
    objects not resembling: *Dundry*
    paper clinging to: *Todwick*
PENS
    felt-tip, dried-up: *Scratby*
    general, dried-up: *Pendomer*
PEOPLE
    anxiously hovering: *Lunning*
    expertly ingratiating: *Polyphant*
    incomprehensibly annoying:
    Goodworth Clatford
    incomprehensibly clever: *Nouster*
    irritatingly chirpy: *Henty*
    not worth meeting: *Eworthy*
    patronisingly dismissive:
    Unsworth
    perfectly inoffensive: *Oulton*
    plumply scurrying: *Chudleigh*
    remarkably well-connected:
    Fifield Bavant
    smug: *Nurney*
PERFUME: *Osmotherley*
PETS
    alarming, unconventional:
    Mastrils
    code of silence among: *Almurta*
    owner-resembling: *Upton*
    Snodsbury

PHALLIC
  not really: *Dundry*
  quite the reverse: *Vange*
PHONE CALLS
  forgetfulness during: *Hoo Hole*
  gestures to invite: *Barlin*
  that suddenly stop: *Frognal*
PHOTOCOPIERS: *Brampton Bierlow*
PICNICS: *Thornton Heath*
PIE CRUSTS: *Crimcrest*
PIERCINGS, genital: *Climping*
PIGEONS, musical: *Aberdovey*
PILLOWS, magical: *Prospidnick*
PIN NUMBERS, theatrical: *Zolling*
PLANNING: *Kyle Lodge*
PLASTERS: *Greinton*
PLOT TWISTS: *Ulceby Skitter*
POCKETS
  bulging: *Nunney*
  patting: *Chettle*
  tiny: *Quarff*
POLICE
  in corner shop: *Derryrush*
  in retirement: *Dunstable*
  not in the car you think they are:
  Coptiviney
POLITICAL INCORRECTNESS:
  Hebden Bridge
PORNOGRAPHY, red-hot:
  Ardateggle
POSES, poncy: *Anembo*
POSTCARDS: *Smailholm*
POTATOES
  actors posing as: *Tubbrid*
  jiggling of roast: *Skeffling*
  tramlines in mashed: *Murroes*
PRATS, jaunty: *Bingley*
PREGNANCY
  environmentally friendly: *Treborth*
  rude exploration of:
  Koolyanobbing
PREMONITIONS: *Dingle*
PRESENTS
  badly-wrapped: *Wookey Hole*
  bits left after wrapping:

  Carnalbanagh Sheddings
  bought for oneself: *Sepon*
  last minute: *Amazonia*
PRETENDING
  to be doing what you said you'd
  do: *Shimpling*
  to text when you aren't really:
  Clavering
PRINCE CHARLES: *Chadbury*
PRINGLES: *Cliasmol*
PRISON, boyfriends in: *Huney*
PROBLEMS, spooky quantum
  fluctuation of: *Michigan*
PROSPECTUSES: *Frobost*
PROSTITUTES, drowned:
  Underriver Ho
PUBIC HAIR
  in teeth: *Gruting*
  in throat: *Throsk*
  traditional: *Winnersh Triangle*
  untraditional: *Mauritius*
PUBS
  Scottish: *McGregor's Corner*
  toilets in: *Sproxton*
  villains in: *Stratford Tony*

Q

QUESTIONS
  indirect: *Horning*
  innocuous: *Penton Mewsey*
  macho: *Prisk*
  rhetorical: *Dargies*
  secret: *Cricklade*
  unanswerable: *Quadring Eaudike*
QUEUES
  airport: *Nedging*
  bastards ahead of you in:
  Straidkilly
  imbecile at the front of:
  Stranagalwilly
  saddos behind you in: *Straidbilly*
QUOTATION MARKS, miming of:
  Ruddle

R

RABBIS: *Klemzig*
RADIATORS: *Noards*
RADIO 4: *Keith Inch, Low Whinnow*
RAKES: *Ebford*
READY MEALS: *Kilwinning*
REALISATIONS, horrible:
    Rackwallace
RECIPES, risky: *Tatlows Folly*
RECTORS: *Sydling St Nicholas*
REFLECTIONS
    attractive, of fellow passengers:
    Eyeworth
    disorienting, of yourself:
    Cockadilly
    misleading, of street lamps:
    Barbican
REMARKS
    bland: *Thursby*
    suggestive: *Cherry Hinton*
REPETITION, unnecessary: *Dublin*
REPETITION, unnecessary: *Dublin*
RESIDUES
    feathery: *Pluckley*
    muffiny: *Remenham*
RESTAURANTS
    fast-food: *Barjarg*
    Japanese: *Nibun*
    people who won't leave:
    Frampton-on-Severn
    touristy: *Barbaggio*
RETCHING: *Muker*
ROSES: *Zigler*
ROUNDABOUTS
    dizziness induced by: *Bodelwyddan*
    unpopular exits from: *Uffcott*
ROYALTY
    boxes of: *Kingledoors*
    exes of: *Cleobury Mortimer*
    ointment of: *Chadbury*
RUBBISH
    all over the café table: *Scurdie
    Ness*

all over the path: *Yardley Gobion*
all over the street: *Spath*
RUGBY
    parents roaring at: *Grangebellew*
    other unseemly oral behaviour in:
    Cockermouth
RUGS, manky: *Hobbister*

S

SANDWICHES
    ejections from: *Cobnash*
    fingerprints on: *Venables*
    vegetarian: *Hay-on-Wye*
SAUSAGES: *Dar es Salaam*
SCHOOL
    enemies: *Old Edlington*
    nostalgia: *Gillygooly*
    photographs: *Drewton*
SCOTSMEN, big: *Big Neeston*
SCRABBLE, bag: *Ae*
SCRUMS: *Cockermouth*
SEALS, non-performing:
    Fugglestone St Peter
SECURITY, false sense of: *Skirling*
SELF-LOATHING
    from eating doughnuts: *Bunratty*
    from surfing the internet: *Fowey*
SENSES, spooky: *Balerno,
    Kanumbra*
SERVANTS
    of mad scientists: *Goltho*
    of Sir Elton John: *Flothers*
SEWELL, BRIAN: *Westby-with-
    Plumptons*
SEX, lacklustre: *Soppog*
SEXUAL POSITIONS
    impractical: *Badgers Mount*
    unwieldy: *Glutton Bridge*
SHACKS, picturesque: *Mill Craig*
SHAKESPEARE
    words coined by: *Cocumont*
    incomprehensible jokes of:
    Pepper Arden Bottoms

SHAVING
expressions: *Gelligroes*
oligarchs: *Mirkady Point*
lacunae: *Donibristle*
scrotums: *Mauritius*
SHEETS
folding: *Chinley*
nylon: *Evercreech*
SHOES
borrowed: *Shunnies*
scratchy: *Crigglestone*
squeaky: *Skeete*
superior: *Menadarva*
wrong: *Wyre Piddle*
SHORT CUTS: *Addison*
SHOULDERS
boyfriends': *Mountnessing*
giants': *Newtonmore*
voids over: *Bannerbank*
SHOWERS
adulterous: *Humbug Scrub*
agonising: *Minterburn*
SHYNESS: *Weesp*
SIDEBURNS, wispy: *Fylingdales*
SIGNATURES, disastrous: *Void-Vacon*
SIGNS
ambiguous: *Toft*
Back In 5 Mins: *Bambill*
bolshy: *Bugle Gate*
Closing Down: *Croth*
driving test: *Toller Whelme*
SILENCE
awkward: *Harpenden*
codes of: *Almurta*
resentful: *Ferring*
SINGER-SONGWRITERS: *Harburn*
SKIING: *Melcombe Horsey*
SKIN
colour: *Pockley*
texture: *Rockness*
SLEEP, sentences read just before: *Audley End*
SMELLS
fishy: *Garstang*

foreign: *Fruence*
woody: *Zezikon*
SMILES, special: *Jilakin*
SMOKERS
al fresco: *Hackenthorpe*
centenarian: *Sproatley*
disapproving coughs at: *Hackforth*
people who claim not to be: *Clonbunny*
SNACKS
twig-based: *Ustibar*
vacuous: *Nantwich*
SNEEZES
blessed aftermath of: *Gdansk*
blissful aftermath of: *Ozleworth*
subcontinental: *Agharoo*
torrential: *Farleaze*
SNORTS
derisive: *Pootings*
exasperated: *Drumnadrochit*
SNOT
dried, in nose: *Corpusty*
dried, on hotel wall: *Drongan*
fresh, in hankie: *Hankerton*
SOAP
tiny noises of: *Thorpe Thewles*
tiny pieces of: *Abcott*
SOCKS
low: *Southerndown*
round: *Tuckton*
sticky: *Greinton*
tight: *Crimcrest*
wet: *Maesog*
SOUVENIRS: *Corlattylannan, Folkestone, Jamberoo*
SPANISH: *Tahila*
SPEECHES, Best Man's: *Prayle Grove*
SPEEDWALKING: *Walkerburn*
SPELLING
uncertain: *Ummeracly*
unclear: *Ruswarp*
SPELLS, unfeasible: *Lancaster*
SPINACH, underestimated: *Grampound*

[205]

SPOONS, undersized: *Stirling*
SPOTS, unsqueezed: *Ulbster*
SPRINTING, unsustainable:
   Springboig
SPRITZERS: *Ffridd Faldwyn*
STAINS
   crotch: *Steg*
   grassy: *Grassy Cletts*
STAIRLIFTS: *Stanway*
STAIRS
   bottom of the: *Ramna Stacks*
   bounding up the: *Ringaskiddy*
STAR TREK: *Peakirk*
STATIONS, whizzing by: *Didcot
   Parkway*
STEPS, lightly running up: *Gailey
   Wharf*
STONES
   rolling: *Rockness*
   significant: *Carrogs*
   tomb: *Hartley Mauditt*
   tossed ineptly: *Hurlet*
STRANGERS
   buffetings from: *Bempton*
   lingering gazes from: *Teddington
   Lock*
STUTTERING: *Termonfeckin*
SUNTANS: *Caramany*
SUPERMARKETS
   alterations in: *Kangy Angy*
   beeping in: *Barcillonnette*
   exotic produce in: *Quatt*
   plastic wedges in: *Tildonk*
   sniffing fruit in: *Grantham*
   snooping in: *Munising*
   unnecessary purchases from:
   Zububa
SWIMMING, euphoria after:
   Stromness
SWIMWEAR: *Swaffham Bulbeck*
SYMPTOMS, complete absence of:
   Asquith

T

T-SHIRTS: *Cleethorpes*
TABLES
   marked by hot mugs: *Sinton*
   piled with other people's mess:
   Scurdie Ness
   wiped lackadaisically: *Plean*
   wonky: *Baltyfarrell*
TACT, complete absence of: *Powfoot*
TALKING, long after you've left the
   room: *Doncaster*
TAMPONS: *Walberswick*
TAPS
   inert (interior): *Tapnage*
   inoperative (exterior):
   Framingham Pigot
TASKS
   more difficult than anticipated:
   Arbuckle Junction
   performed with mute resentment:
   Ferring
TAXI DRIVERS: *Gerzat*
TAXIS
   imaginary: *Barbican*
   waiting outside: *Thurrock*
TEA
   detecting inferior: *Te'ekiu*
   manoeuvring inferior: *Teesside*
   offering inferior: *Teetz*
   suspecting inferior: *Teevurcher*
TEARS
   chess-induced: *King's Pyon*
   film-induced: *Bweeng*
   walk-induced: *Wendover*
TEENAGERS
   awkward: *Quambone*
   diseased: *Kirk Smeaton*
   French: *Clignancourt*
   in bedroom: *Oodnadatta*
   inexplicable: *Woomera*
TEETH
   food visible in: *Cloghogle*
   pubic hair caught in: *Gruting*

TELEVISION
denial of watching: *Wonersh*
eating while watching: *Volimes*
inability to do without: *Boxworth*
inability to switch off: *Troon*
interminable interludes on: *Hanging Langford*
rubbishy old films on: *Cruntully*
rubbishy spin-offs on: *Butt of Lewis*
Scandinavian: *Skallary*
swearing at: *Voorst*
TENNIS
balls: *Nibun*
games: *Boyanup*
ladders: *Aberlemno*
nets: *Ness of Tenston*
TERMS AND CONDITIONS: *Dadlesmere*
TESTICLES: *Baffle*
TEXTING
inattentive: *Wiveliscombe*
misdirected: *Wroxeter*
simulated: *Clavering*
thwarted: *Yàmbol*
THINGS
half-sucked: *Annecy*
left behind in a rush: *Hastings*
that go round and round: *Sorrento*
that haven't started yet: *Ings*
THRIFT: *Eakring*
TICKLING
immunity to: *Inverarish*
infantile: *Killybegs*
TIES: *Fiskerton*
TIGHTS: *Aughnaloopy*
TILLS: *Barcillonnette*
TIME, mysterious nature of: *Ebberston*
TINS
biscuit: *Cruggion*
grandmotherly: *Biscathorpe*
roasting: *Rishangles*
TIPPING

gauging reaction to: *Skeeby*
uncertainty over: *Ormskirk*
TIREDNESS, happy: *Malmö*
TOAST: *Brulange*
TOASTERS: *Largs*
TODDLERS
anti-social: *Pootilla*
ooze from: *Hanging Grimston*
TOENAILS: *Evercreech*
TOILET PAPER
cheap: *Fingal's Cave*
Greek: *Plocrapool*
TOILETS
disabled: *Bowshank*
Japanese: *Ando*
literary: *Dunning*
occupied: *Arbroath*
symbolic: *Praze-an-Beeble*
TOMBSTONES: *Hartley Mauditt*
TONGUES, scraped with a spoon: *Muker*
TOOLBELTS: *Llandrillo*
TOOLS
imaginary: *Jeffcott*
small, pointy: *Fugglestone St Peter*
TOURISTS: *Barbaggio, Clignancourt*
TOWELS
dry bits of: *Crotone*
fluffiness of: *Abernethy*
on women's heads: *Curbans*
used as bathmats: *Uralla*
TOYS
expensively designed by Swiss: *Zaltbommel*
hideously disfigured by dogs: *Kuala Lumpur*
TRAFFIC, nervous: *Coptiviney*
TRAFFIC JAMS, walking about sighing in: *Norristhorpe*
TRAFFIC LIGHTS, mysterious lack of power over: *Wilberfoss*
TRAINS: *Didcot Parkway*
TRAMPS: *Brompton Ralph*

Trees, climbing: *Oakhanger*
Trousers
  cricketing: *Grassy Cletts*
  high-waisted: *Boffles*
  loopy: *Keetmanshoop*
Trumpet, nose blown like a: *Honeybugle*
Truncheons: *Kettletoft*
Tubing: *Thil*
Tyres
  obstacle: *Salterhebble*
  screeching: *Vereeniging*
Twats, monumental: *The Knab*
Twins: *Twinhoe*
Twitching: *Barooga*
Twitter
  envy: *Snaith*
  gluttony: *Tweefontein*
  lust: *Twitchen*
  pride: *Tootgarook*

U

Ultrasound: *Geurie*
Ulysses: *Ullinish*
Undertakers: *Creevins*
Unmentionables, pristine: *Primrose Valley*
Urination
  female, *al fresco*: *Gussage All Saints*
  male, *al fresco*: *North Piddle*
  one-eyed: *Slaithwaite*

V

Vegetables
  chopped: *Gerrots*
  improbable lust for: *Loughborough*
  unlikely: *Zumpango*
Vegetarianism: *Duckend Green, Hay-On-Wye*

Vicars
  who are in the wrong job: *Abbots Ripton*
  who ride motorcycles: *Viker*
Views
  reflected: *Menangle*
  rural: *Balmaha*
Virgin Mary: *Macerata, Stocklinch Magdalen*
Viruses, *see* **Jeffrey Archer**
Voices
  lifty: *Gwennap*
  witchy: *Wychling*
  womenish: *Quarles*

W

Waiters
  Italian, impressive: *Bringolo*
  Italian, overattentive: *Askamore*
Waiting rooms: *Asquith*
Wakefulness, dubious: *Dorney*
Walks
  country, ending in cannibalism: *Dibden Purlieu*
  country, ending in tears: *Wendover*
  country, ending in walking further: *Heddon*
  urban, circuitous: *Lizard Siding*
Walls: *Woll*
War Rooms, the little rakes in: *Ebford*
Warts: *Moy*
Washing Machines
  quiet clinking of: *Colston Bassett*
  violent shuddering of: *Halamanning*
Water, other people's tepid: *Bawtry*
Waves
  feeble: *Whimble*
  Mexican: *Manjimup*
Waxing, enthusiastic: *Tinkerbush*
Wedgies: *Lower Sheering*

WELLIES
mud on: *Cumberland*
removal of: *Heddle*
socks in: *Southerndown*
WHISKS, gilded: *Flothers*
WIND, breaking: *Farthinghoe*
WINDOWS
aeroplane: *Frasseto*
attractive people reflected in:
Eyeworth
car: *Croome*
rattling: *Shap*
walking into: *Shackerstone*
WINDSCREENS
furious notes on:
Derrynacuheragh
interesting shapes on: *Scudellate*
scraping ice off: *Carlton Scroop*
WINE, people who pretend to know
about: *Wendling*
WINSTONE, RAY: *Levitt Hagg*
WOMEN
addressed as guys: *Barnave*
crying in unison: *Quatremare*
who are expensively thin: *Miskin*
who must be mythical: *Woumen*
who want something: *Quarles*
WOODLICE: *Carnoustie*
WOODS: *Sticklepath*
WORDS
disconcertingly misread:
Youlgreave
newly-encountered: *Stocklinch
Ottersey*
Shakespearean: *Cocumont*
unspellable: *Warlus*
weird-looking: *Worb*
WORK, futile: *Dorking*
WORKMEN, feckless: *Jeffcott*
WORRIES, nocturnal: *Zouch*
WRISTBANDS: *Jamberoo*
WRISTWATCHES: *Wychbold*

X

X: *Xining*

Y

YAWNS
injuries caused by: *Yarborough*
interruptions prompted by:
Kewstoke
YELLS, weedy: *Carnforth*
YOUTUBE: *Sorrento*

Z

ZONES, erogenous: *The Pole of
Itlaw*
ZOYS, whatever they might be:
Middlezoy

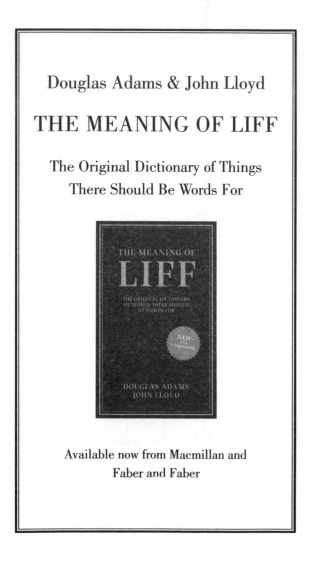